1750	1780	1790	1810
1700	1770	1790	1820
1670	1700	1740	1780
1650	1750	1800	1810

ANTIQUES

ANTIQUES

BY
SARAH M. LOCKWOOD

*TEXT ILLUSTRATIONS
BY*
ERNEST STOCK

*WRAPPER AND LINING DRAWINGS
BY*
ILONKA KARASZ

GARDEN CITY   NEW YORK
DOUBLEDAY, DORAN & COMPANY, INC.
1928

COPYRIGHT, 1925, BY DOUBLEDAY, PAGE
& COMPANY. ALL RIGHTS RESERVED.
PRINTED IN THE UNITED STATES AT THE
COUNTRY LIFE PRESS, GARDEN CITY, N. Y.

ANTIQUES

ANTIQUES

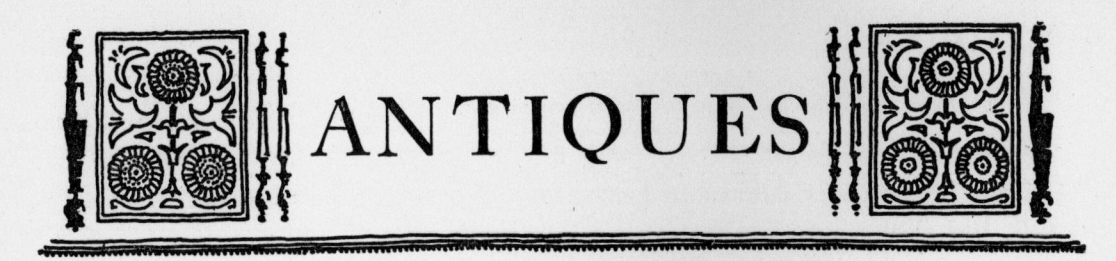

THIS book is written for people who are interested in Early American Furniture, not so much from a collector's point of view—although we like to collect, too, so far as we are able—but because we have found out recently how much we like the old things and how nice it is to have them with us in our homes. In fact, there are a great many of us to-day, all over America, who would like nothing better than a real old-fashioned American home. The only trouble is, it has been such a long time since we have had one that we are just a bit hazy about what it is like. For a great many years now the furniture of our forefathers has been out of fashion; shoved into the background by factory-made "Period" stuff, swamped under the "Mission" deluge and such-like notions that have changed too rapidly for us to remember that up in the attic and out in the barn are the fine sturdy pieces that stood by our Colonial fathers while they were making a nation for us.

To-day, with the swift enthusiasm with which America does everything, we want them back. We want them all back. Nothing is too crude or simple to be untouched by the glamour that our tardy affection pours out upon them. We clasp them all, good, bad, and indifferent, to our bosoms with beaming smiles. But back of it all is a slight uneasiness as to just who these old friends are. Their faces are familiar but we can't remember their names.

As a matter of fact, it is not difficult to find out. The subject of Early American Furniture is not an exhaustive one. It covers only a short period of time—from 1620 to about 1850. During that time we were too busy snaking stumps out of the ground, fighting savages, and pulling off a war of Independence to make such a lot of furniture. That is to say, it is no such subject as English or French or Italian furniture is to the people of those countries, and yet they seem to be able to understand theirs and to furnish their homes in their own traditions.

ANTIQUES

The object of this book is to re-introduce us to our old friends; to skim from as broad a surface as we can as many of the outstanding facts as we can that have to do with Early American Furniture. No one subject has been treated in detail, but many subjects have been touched upon as clearly and briefly as possible, giving sound information as far as it goes and leading the way to further study in the fine big books that are listed in the back of this one.

It is obvious that in treating the subject as broadly as this we shall have to be as compact and exact as possible. The simplest way to do this is to arrange our subjects alphabetically, but just because it takes that form do not look upon it, please, as a glossary. It is nothing like as complete as that. It is just a Primer of A B C's, with pictures and stories to help fix the big facts in our memories and to lay the foundation in a comfortable, workable way for an agreeable acquaintance with American antiques.

A

Beauty is truth, truth beauty,—that is all
Ye know on earth, and all ye need to know.
—Keats: "Ode on a Grecian Urn."

"A" STARTS us off with ADAM, a hard nut to crack, but one you must know something about right from the beginning, for the influence of this man, far-reaching, penetrating, and characteristic, affected, directly or indirectly, many architectural and furniture forms in our country. Therefore, the first man is ADAM.

There were four brothers Adam. The greatest of these was Robert. His influence on the furniture of England from 1760 to 1780 was very marked. A man of culture and ample means. A traveller. An architect, designer, and decorator. He was not a cabinet maker. He never made a stick of furniture in his life, although, strangely enough, it is upon his furniture that his fame rests to-day. When he designed a house he also designed the furniture to go into it, even going so far as to mark with chalk the spot on the floor where each piece was to stand. Adam's designs were painstaking, exquisite in the spirit of antiquity. He drew his inspiration direct from ancient Pompeii uninfluenced by his trip through France. His lines were straight, his legs consistently so, his backs round or oval. His decoration was purely classic; he often employed the well-known "Classic Urn." He delighted in satinwood, highly finished and partially painted. Some of his panels, done by famous painters, are masterpieces in themselves. Of course, he also designed for mahogany, and for baser woods entirely painted; but it is in light wood, airy and graceful, that we find the real Adam. Adam's furniture was actually made in the shops of Chippendale, Hepplewhite, and other cabinet makers of the day who sometimes had to modify his designs to make them practical. Naturally, some of the beauty of the designs stuck to the fingers of the makers, thereby causing the confusion that has agitated the expert ever since. It will never be known just how much Hepplewhite owed to Adam, and certainly some of his ideas came to full flower in the masterpieces of Sheraton, whose

ANTIQUES

influence in turn was so deeply felt over here. For example, we find much Adam (via Sheraton) in the work of Duncan Phyfe.

There we have Adam, a painstaking, rather priggish gentleman, formal, cold, and a bit stand-offish with his men, if we may judge his character from his furniture, which certainly isn't warm, but then the purely classic never is. And he may have snubbed old Chippendale, for while it is probable that many of his designs were executed in that shop, not one trace of Adam's influence is in the old man's work. Strange, too, for Chippendale in his time made good use of everything that came his way. Perhaps the old master resented the rising of a new star on the horizon. At any rate, Adam brought about a sharp change in furniture styles, and it will help a great deal as we go along if we will remember this.

B

Let his bed be hard, and rather Quilts than Feathers. Hard lodging strengthens the Parts, whereas being buried every night in Feathers melts and dissolves the Body.

—John Locke.

"B" OF course, starts with BEDS, a rather wide subject, but not difficult to clear up. The bed *stead* is the frame upon which the bedding is placed, and it is interesting to see how its form has changed as living conditions changed. The ancient bed of northern Europe, from which our own bed is evolved, was a huge wooden affair entirely enclosed in panels. It had a roof and everything, like a little room within a room. When the occupants, several in number, crawled into it and closed the sliding panels, they were completely protected from the icy wind that whistled through the open windows. This was around 1050. As the living conditions improved the side panels were replaced by heavy curtains, but the back panel and the heavy wooden top were kept. These were the huge carved beds of Queen Elizabeth's and Jacobean times. Then in 1700 the back panel and roof went, leaving the four posts which supported a wooden cornice from which the curtains hung.

These beds were still ponderous affairs, enormously wide so that some of the children as well as the parents could share the warmth of the curtains and billowy feather bedding. The fireplace and the bed were the only warm spots in the house, and the best sprinter got the best place. By 1750 the wooden cornice was often replaced by a valance.

It was at this time that the four-poster reached its finest expression. The graceful draperies were no longer a dire necessity, but were hung to enhance the beauty of the bed, the handsome carved posts dignified in rich brocade, the simple ones dainty in muslin with knotted fringe. By 1800 the draperies were gone, leaving four high posts, naked as totem poles. Then the four posts were cut down shorter and shorter until at last, with the Empire in 1830, they entirely disappeared, the head- and footboards came back, and we have the familiar modern bedstead.

ANTIQUES 6

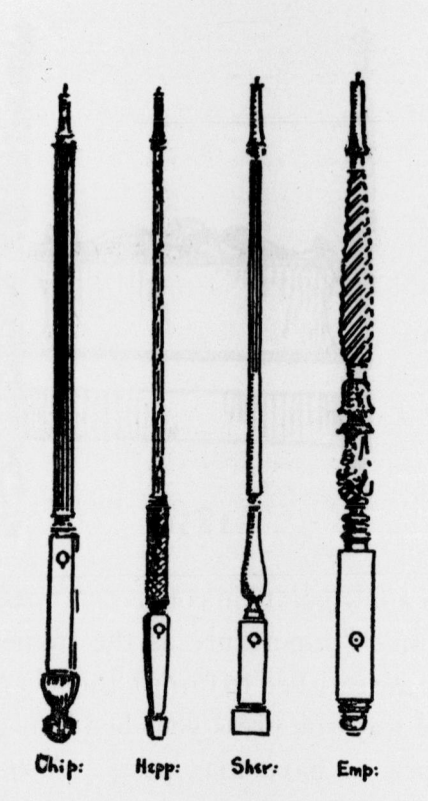

Field Bedstead

Chip: Hepp: Sher: Emp:

EARLY AMERICAN BEDSTEADS—As a matter of fact, no really early beds have survived to tell the tale. We know they had them, because after 1645 "bedsteads and vallents" are constantly turning up in the inventories. Some of them must have been the heavy panelled type brought over from England. Many of them were just frames on which to lay bedding, and some of them, called "Presse" beds, were built into the houses so that they could be lifted up and fastened against the wall when not in use. Bedsteads are clumsy, and probably the old ones were destroyed as soon as the newer types came in.

FIELD BED—One of the earliest as well as the simplest beds that have come down to us is the charming "Field" bed, dating from about 1750. This was made of maple, pine, or cherry with slender, simply turned posts with an arched or "sprung" frame at the top over which the net canopy was thrown. These were also called "Tent" beds, because of the canopy being arched up instead of straight. These beds, hung with simple draperies edged with the knotted fringe so popular at that time, are the most delightful and typical of the Colonial beds. They were popular for many years; in fact, until four-posters went out for good, so that fortunately they are still to be found. . . . The Field bed is typically American, but there were many four-posters here, either imported from England or made after English designs, that were dignified and beautiful. The so-called Chippendale bed with handsomely carved footposts with ball-and-claw feet is very fine. Usually the two head posts are not carved because they were concealed by drapery and there are beds where all four posts are not carved for that same reason. Women took much pride in their draperies, spending hours of patient needlework upon them, and very gorgeous and important they were, too. By 1780 much of the heavy drapery was left off and all four slender posts were delicately carved or reeded in the manner of Hepplewhite or Sheraton. By 1810 the deadly influence of the Empire began to creep in. Posts became heavier, the carving coarser—acanthus leaves, pineapple leaves and fruit, heavy twists and flutings massed together in meaningless jumble. By 1825 the draperies were gone and the tops of the posts finished in a flourishing pineapple. Gradually the posts were cut down, and the head- and footboards were replaced. These were called the "Half-headed" beds. They were often made in maple or birch or cherry, and, when the four posts are nicely carved, are attractive, if somewhat heavy, beds. They are easily found. About 1840 the posts were left off entirely and the foot- and headboards gracefully curved. These are called "Sleigh beds" because of their shape. They remained popular until 1850. After this there were many simple beds with spool turnings and low peaked head- and footboards. They can still be picked up by the dozen in any countryside, and when painted make delightful beds.

1789

1830

Before we leave beds let us clear up a few points in connection with them. The furnishing of an old bed is of as much importance as the frame. Too many people who have fine old bedsteads are satisfied to furnish them in modern draperies. As a matter of fact, it is the way you dress your bed that gives it character, not the fact that you happen to have four posts. Also, many people look for old single beds. There were no such beds. The only thing that approached it was the "Trundle or Truckle bed" on wheels, that children slept in and that in the daytime was rolled under the big bed—that, and the "Angel" bed, a plain frame without posts. The only way to get "old-fashioned" single beds is, quite frankly, to have them made. Of course, the factory finish sticks out all over them.

In the old days the housewife's pride was to pile her costly feather beds on top of one another as far as she was able. The consequence was one needed steps to climb in. "Bed steps" are interesting from a historical point of view, but I do not see much sense in putting them beside a modern mattress. In fact, I do not like any forced or unnatural use of old things. I particularly hate to see, as I have seen more than once beside a fireplace, a sweet old cradle, filled with wood!

BUREAUS are a hybrid piece of furniture combining the duties of a chest of drawers and a dressing table, most uncomfortable to stand up to and hard to light. The word "bureau" really means desk (as, for example, in the expression, "bureau of information,") and it is only in America that these pieces of furniture are called bureaus. In England they are "chests of drawers." After Hepplewhite came along, about 1770, high-boys went out and bureaus came in. They are really chests of drawers with their proportions and contour changed.

BUREAU FORMS—The block front was among the first of the new designs and was popular on desks as well as bureaus. It was made by carving the thick mahogany boards that made the front into block form, two blocks raised and one in the middle depressed. . . . When the edges of the raised blocks curved off into the centre depression it was a true block front. . . . When these edges were left square it was a square front. . . . When the blocks gave way to a sweeping out-and-in curve it was a serpentine front. . . . When the curve swelled gently toward the centre it was a swell front, and when the two lower drawers bulged out at the front and sides it was a kettle front—all obviously descriptive and all made about the same time. . . . The "chests of drawers," usually with the swell or serpentine front, made by Hepplewhite and Sheraton in light mahogany veneer, delicately inlaid, with French feet and oval brass mounts are the finest of these bureaus. . . . A handsome mirror was usually hung above such a piece, or a little "dressing glass" stood upon it. These delicate glasses, made to swing in a frame with tiny drawers beneath for smaller articles of toilet, are lovely, especially those made by Sheraton, dainty in

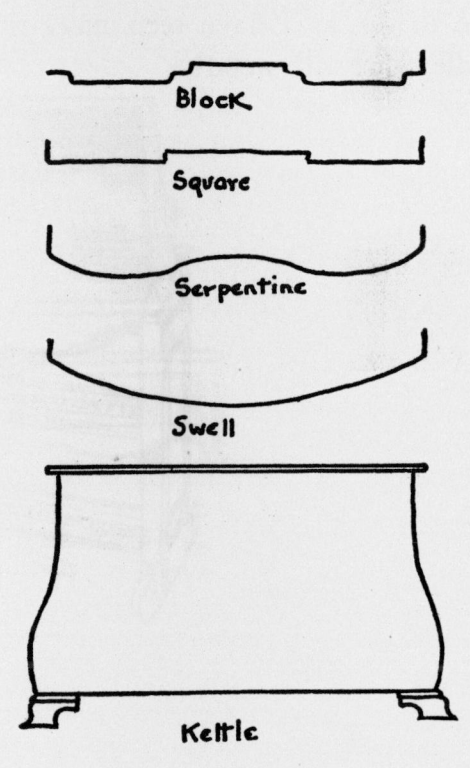

ANTIQUES

Swell Front Bureau

design and daintily inlaid. . . . Then, with the coming of the everlasting "Empire," the bureau fronts got straight and square with heavily carved uprights on either side. The little dressing glasses, with everything else, gradually grew heavier and coarser. The drawers were made larger, and there were two tiers of them instead of one. . . . They were attached to the bureau top—and there you have the familiar bureau that has persisted ever since.

Dressing Glass

C

*The chest, contriv'd a double debt to pay,—
A bed by night, a chest of drawers by day.*
—GOLDSMITH: "The Deserted Village."

"C" MUST begin with CHIPPENDALE, the most outstanding and powerful figure in the history of furniture making. It is curious that the only men who ever stamped their names upon furniture types should have lived and worked together at the same time and in the same place, but so it is. Chippendale, Adam, Hepplewhite, and Sheraton (we shall call these the "Big Four" from now on, for convenience' sake) all lived in London and brought their work to perfection there between 1750 and 1800. Remember that. And remember, also, that the first of these, not only in years but in power of personality, was Chippendale.

CHIPPENDALE was born about 1705 and died in 1779. The son of a country wood carver and cabinet maker, he came to London in 1727, and, by his forceful personality and shrewdness in making himself liked by the right people, soon built up a large clientèle. His shop became a fashionable rendezvous for great lords and ladies who came there mornings to titter about the scandals at Court and to vie with each other in buying furniture. Chippendale was not above adding a touch of spice to the gossip and making the most of the ensuing good humour—so much carving, so much cash—and it was probably to please rich clients with more money than good taste that he executed some of his over-ornate pieces. His finest expression is in what might be called his "inexpensive" work. Chippendale, besides being a master carver and designer, was also a good advertiser. Somehow, in thinking of him Barnum always comes to mind, for although men had been making furniture for centuries, Chippendale was the first to impress his name upon his work. Chippendale's style was frankly derived from various sources—the Dutch, the French, the Chinese, etc.—but he put such a wealth of individuality into everything he touched that the original source is lost in a style entirely his own. There is

ANTIQUES

something thoroughly English about his work, something sturdy and honest: the broad comfy seat, the stout back, the straight legs or else jolly bandy "Uncle Toby" ones that could come from nowhere in the world but "Merrie England." A big man who made big furniture, he held England in the hollow of his hand for thirty years. . . . Then Adam, Hepplewhite, and Sheraton came along with their straight lines, light woods, and airy decorations, and Chippendale's bandy legs and heavy carving were pushed into the background.

CHAIRS are the most tricky, temperamental, and versatile members of the furniture family—and by far the most important. They are the most numerous and varied of all household furnishings, and they are the first to lend themselves to the whims of fashion or vagaries of the cabinet maker. No wonder the subject slips and slides, overlapping, interchanging in a most bewildering way. Just the same, like most difficulties, they are not half so bad as you think they are when you once get right at them. We will do this by first explaining certain chair terms that appear in every description of them, and then dividing the chairs themselves into two groups: the early Colonial chairs and those that came under the influence of the "Big Four." We will start off, then, with the chair terms.

TURNINGS—Pieces of wood that have been turned on a lathe. The simplest form of carving, very much used on early furniture. The turnings took many forms according to the fancy of the man who held the chisel—either very simple as on the early chairs, or elaborated into cups and sausage, trumpet and bell shapes. Often the cup and "trumpet" are inverted and elongated into a sort of vase motif. These turnings were particularly used on our earliest pieces before the Dutch bandy leg came in. Sometimes they ended in a ball foot or a squashed bun or a Spanish foot carved into a sort of hoof shape with grooves, or, more elaborate still, the Flemish scroll—a longish "S" scroll.

THE DUTCH BANDY or cabriole leg came in right after the turnings, about 1725. It curved out from the chair seat in a more or less pronounced bulge, ending in a broad flat foot, something like a golf club. . . . Sometimes it was raised on a little disc. . . . Later on the club foot was enlarged into a ball and was carved to look like a

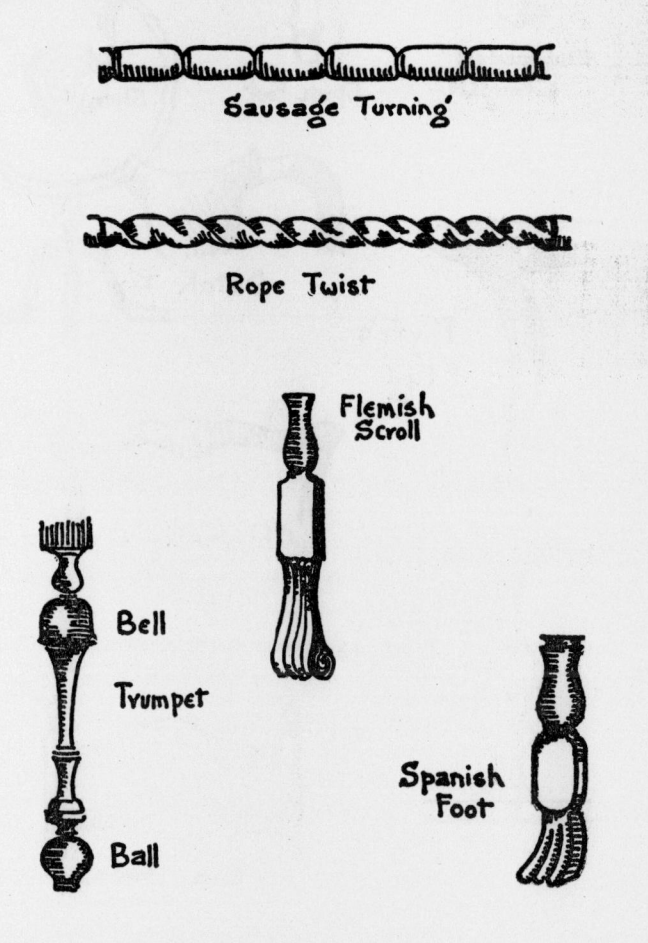

ANTIQUES

Bandy *Ball+Claw* *Snake Foot*

Chippendale Straight *Spade Foot* *Sheraton*

Phyfe's Leg *Dutch Top*

Chippendale

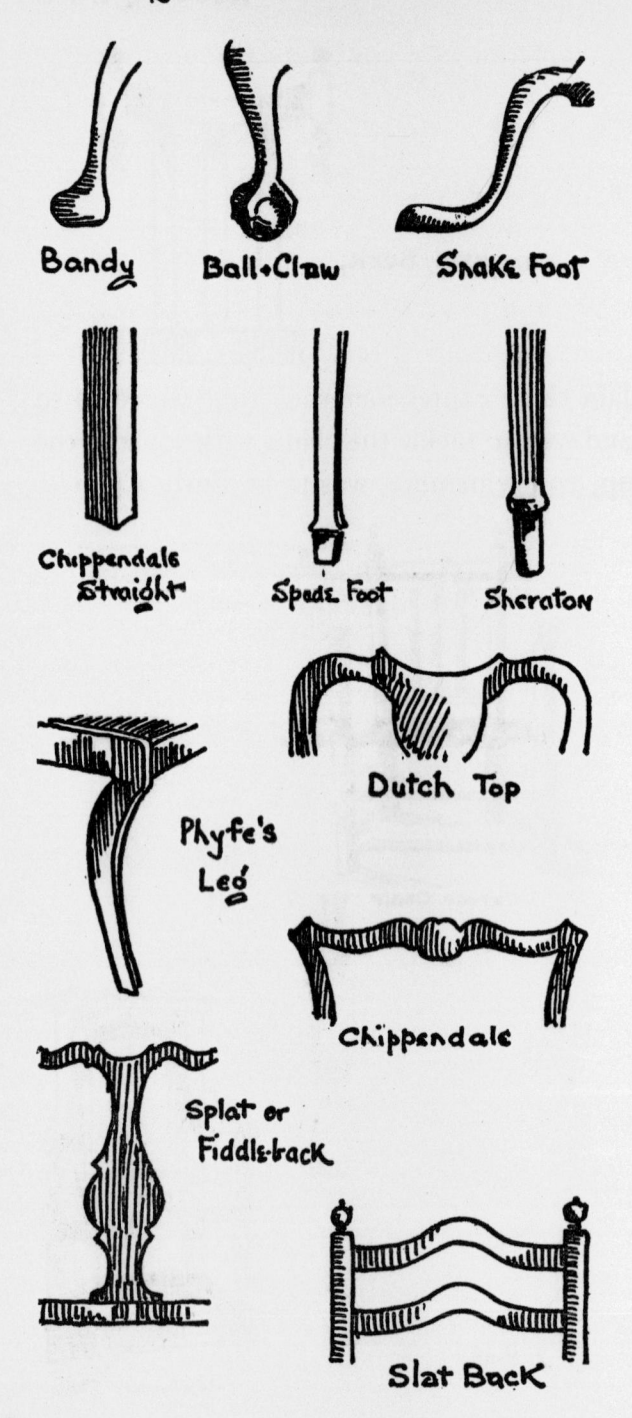

Splat or Fiddle-back

Slat Back

bird's or an animal's claw grasping a ball—the familiar bandy leg with the ball-and-claw foot. . . . Sometimes on delicate pieces like tea tables or candle stands, the foot was elongated to look like a snake's head.

THE STRAIGHT LEG of Hepplewhite and Sheraton was slender and tapering, sometimes ending in a little collar, or widening of the leg about an inch from the floor, called a "spade" foot. . . . Sheraton also used a round straight leg carved with long vertical ridges called "reeding," ending in a little plain turning that tapered delicately to the floor. Sometimes these legs were fitted with dainty brass castors.

Phyfe in 1810 used a long, down-swinging concave curve on his table and chair legs, accentuating it with rows of reeding. This "curule" leg had also been much used by Adam, and it continued long into the Empire period.

TOP RAIL—In early Dutch chairs the top rail curved down smoothly into the side pieces, in shape almost exactly like the yoke carried by the Dutch milkmaids. . . . With Chippendale this yoke often turned up at the ends like a Cupid's bow.

SPLAT BACK—A rather wide vase-shaped panel, either plain or pierced, rising from the seat to the top rail. Found on Queen Anne and Dutch chairs. Called a "fiddle back" in America.

SLAT BACK—Three to five horizontal slats, their upper edges sometimes curved. An early and familiar Colonial back. Sometimes called a "ladder" back.

BANISTER BACK—Several up-and-down slats, like a stair banister. Another well-known back. Used on elaborate as well as on simple chairs.

WINDSOR BACK—Several spindles rising from a wooden seat to a curved top rail.

Bannister Back

Now we will not have to explain these expressions each time we come to them, which will be continuously, and we can tackle the chairs with some of the haze cleared away. The first group, you remember, was to be Early Chairs.

CARVER CHAIR—The earliest chair we have; so called from the one brought over on the *Mayflower* by Governor Carver. A heavy, dignified big chair made entirely of turnings fitted into each other horizontally and vertically. A similar chair but with finer turnings was owned at the same time by Deacon Brewster, and most early turned chairs of that massive type have been called by one or the other of these names ever since. . . . These chairs bring up more vividly than any other piece of furniture a vision of the Puritan Fathers. Sometimes the arms finish in a flat "mushroom" turning that looks as if it had been squashed flat by the weight of the heavy fist that lay upon it.

WAINSCOT CHAIR—Another very early type imported from England. Very heavy, made entirely of oak with solid panel back and seat—hence the name wainscot. Sometimes elaborately carved like the cupboards and chests. Went out with the 17th Century.

FIDDLE BACKS—The familiar and popular early Dutch chair made of

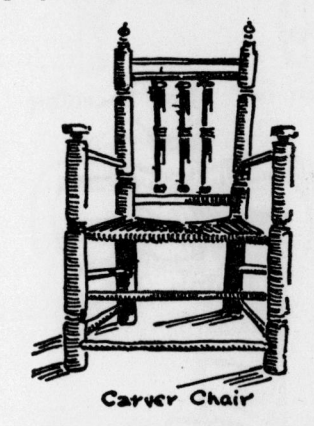

Carver Chair

Wainscot Chair

Fiddle-back

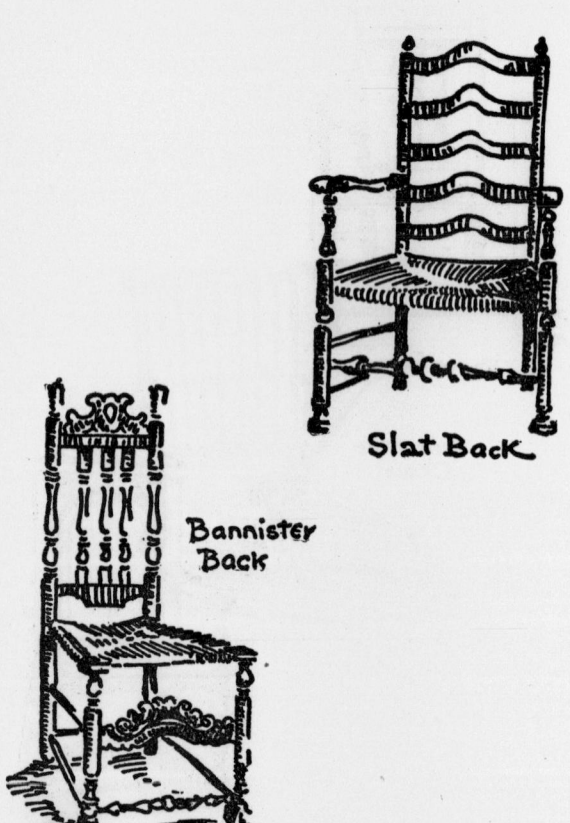

Slat Back

Bannister Back

native wood: maple, ash, hickory, etc., two or three woods often combined. They had the Dutch yoke top rail and plain splat, rush seats and either straight, turned, or slightly "bandy" legs with club feet.

SLAT BACK—Another familiar chair that came in about 1700. Made everywhere all through the Colonies, and may still be found. Those found in Pennsylvania are the most desirable, for they have the tops of the slats curved and the slats bent to fit the back of the sitter. Those with five slats are the best—and hardest to find. They were made of native wood and the legs and back uprights were simply turned. . . . It was to one of these slat backs that Benjamin Franklin attached a pair of rockers sometime around 1750, thereby starting the American rocker on its mad career. . . . Sometimes the slat back was made with two seats and very short legs. These were used in wagons and are called "wagon" chairs. . . . There is no nicer chair to-day for the country porch or breakfast table than the good old slat back.

BANISTER BACK—Came in about the same time as the slat back. Never was a comfortable chair, being high and narrow. Sometimes the banisters were plain, sometimes they were turnings split in two with the smooth side toward the front. Sometimes they were rather elaborately carved about the top rail with caning in the backs and seats and with Spanish feet; a sort of parlour chair, which the slat back never was.

WINDSOR CHAIR—Even more popular and characteristically American than the slat back. They were made from 1740 until 1820. It is said that there were fourteen Windsors on the porch at Mount Vernon. They first appeared in Philadelphia and were immediately popular. Other localities copied them, adding, as usual, their own touches, but fundamentally all Windsors are the same. They are made of combinations of woods: hickory, ash, pine, etc., the seats shaped from a solid piece and the turned legs set into it, raking sharply outward. The backs are made of slender spindles set into the solid seat and rising to the top bent rail. The shapes of these backs differ somewhat. There are hoop backs and loop backs and fan backs, according to the spread of the spindles. The most charming variation was the comb-back, an extension above the middle of the top rail that looks like a comb and which forms a head rest. Sometimes a candle shelf or a writing shelf was attached to the right arm, and it is said that Thomas Jefferson wrote the Declaration of Independence in one of these chairs.

BOSTON ROCKERS—About 1820 rockers were added to the Windsor chair, the wooden seat curved up in the back and a wide top rail added, making the familiar Boston rocker. . . . Windsors were painted green, but the Boston rocker was usually black with a charming bit of stencilling on the headboard. They are the most "comfy" wooden chairs ever made. I remember one with short tippy rockers —an early one—with a "Turkey work" cushion on the seat—— Oh, well!—To go back to Windsors. . . . It is said that they were named after the town in England where they originated, but the English Windsor is entirely different from the American

Comb-back Windsor

Windsor Chair

ANTIQUES

Boston Rocker.

Hitchcock Chair

one, being made of oak and having a pierced splat in the centre of the spindles at the back—the type of Windsor you see in hotel lobbies and club rooms. Not to be confused or compared for a moment with the delightful Philadelphia Windsor.

HITCHCOCK CHAIR—About the time the Colonial Windsor began to go out in 1820-30, there appeared a popular chair that filled in the transition between Colonial times and the Empire. It is called the Hitchcock chair. It is said that Hitchcock was a Yankee from Kennebunkport, Maine, who was originally a ship's carpenter and a painter of figureheads. He and his boys started making chairs, turning them out on a lathe, making the rush seats and doing the stencilling themselves. It is said that they peddled their chairs about the country in a wagon. Whether this is true I do not know, but I do know the chairs are charming. They are usually painted black with the turnings on the legs and uprights picked out in gold. The top half of the back uprights is shaved down to a flat surface, and they are bent slightly and gracefully back. The top rail and the one fancy slat across the back are delightfully stencilled in gold and silver fruits and flowers. It is said that Hitchcock protected the stencils with a thin coat of shellac and that is the reason we often find them so little worn. For we do find these chairs, and a worthwhile find they are, too.

EMPIRE CHAIRS—There were many charming chairs made while Hitchcock was making his. We will speak of Phyfe's later on, for he really deserves a place with the "Big Four." . . . The familiar Empire chairs were small, and much the same in general character. They had a wide top rail and either one vase-like splat or one plain or fancy cross-wise slat. The most charming of them were made of curly maple with cane or rush seats, and they are still very often found in sets of six or more. The mahogany ones of the same time usually had "slip" seats, covered with velvet or horsehair. Sometimes there was a little bunch of roses or leaves carved in the top. These chairs are rather carelessly called "Empire," but they are entirely different from the European chairs of that period, especially those made in our own native maple. I wish we could find some name of our own for our own things. Mr. Walter A. Dyer calls these chairs "Jeffersonian," and I like it.

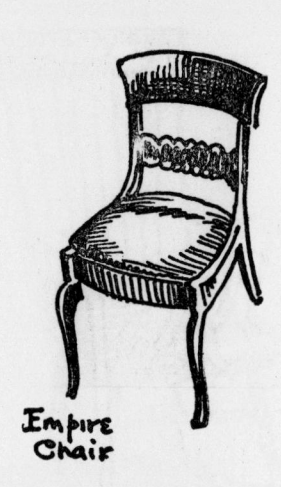

Empire Chair

That, in a general way, covers the early chairs, or rather those that do not come directly under the influence of the "Big Four." Of course, each of these types has endless variations, but these are the outstanding characteristics. Now for the handsomer, richer chairs that came in with Chippendale about 1750. But one thing before we begin: Very, very little of the so-called Chippendale, Hepplewhite, and Sheraton furniture found in America came from the workshops of those men. We know of some examples that are originals, but when people speak of Chippendale, Hepplewhite, or Sheraton furniture they mean pieces that were made by English or American workmen after the designs or more or less in the manner of these men. An American Chippendale chair, for example, is much less ornate than its English prototype, and, to my mind, much lovelier.

CHIPPENDALE began work in London in 1727, and for twenty-five years, until Adam came along, he held sway both in England and over here. In 1753, when he was in the full flush of his popularity, he brought out his book of designs, "The Gentleman and Cabinet Maker's Director." I think now that we have come to the chairs of the big men we will give most of our attention to their backs, for by their backs ye shall know them. Very few chairs

ANTIQUES

are pure-bred. Even the masters borrowed a leg here, a foot there, but no matter how polyglot a chair may be it is the back that determines its type. Remember, too, that Chippendale worked entirely in mahogany, and the only decoration he used was his elaborate and beautiful carving.

Ribbon-back

Ladderback

CHIPPENDALE'S BACKS—Chippendale began by using the Dutch back, generously broadened out and with the top rail bent into a Cupid's bow. Sometimes the ends of the bow were turned down into the uprights as in a true Dutch chair, but more often they finished upward in a little curve. The central splat so far had been plain or with just a simple design cut into it, but Chippendale pounced on it and made it, not only the keynote to his chairs, but perhaps the most characteristic detail of all his work. He always kept pretty much to the old vase shape but within that outline he poured out his imagination in a wealth of designs, some of them simple, some of them involved intertwinings of "ribbons" and "C" curves and Gothic figures almost past belief. There is a never-ending variety to Chippendale's beautiful splat backs. They have been a gold mine for designers ever since. Nobody ever carved as that man did, and when you add to the elaborateness of the back much fine carving on the knees and feet of his cabriole legs you get an extremely handsome chair. . . . He also used perfectly square straight legs, not tapering at all, and these he left severely plain, which in its way enhanced the beauty of the backs even more.

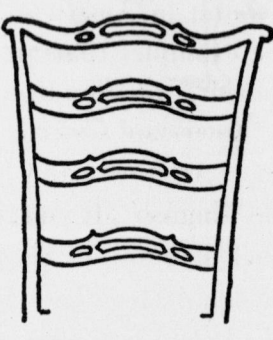

LADDER BACKS—A second favourite design was based upon the slat idea and consisted of three or four wavy ribbon-like horizontals carved to match the top rail. These are called "Chippendale Ladder backs." . . . He also turned to good use the craze for furniture in the Oriental manner, and pieces in this style are called "Chinese Chippendale." Some of his admirers regret this phase as being too faddy and over-ornate. I must say he gave the Chinese idea a run for its money, and it has never come back since. Some of his furniture in that manner is certainly to be regretted, but the lovely chair backs filled from corner to corner with delicate fretwork are worth all his flouncings in the other pieces. . . . The big upholstered fireside chairs made in Chippendale's time were comfortable and extremely graceful in proportion. In the days when the only heat in the room was from the fireplace these chairs, with their wide friendly wings, were well called "EASY CHAIRS." . . .

ROUNDABOUTS—This odd erratic member of the chair family had been around for some time, and, of course, Chippendale made these too after his own manner. It was just a square chair turned cornerwise, with a leg in front, one on each side, and one in the back. The corners were usually rounded and the low back rail supported on three uprights from the three corners. It was popular until about 1770.

Fret-back

Roundabout Chair

There in a broad way you have "Chippendale" backs. If you see a chair of generous proportions, in mahogany, with a back like any of these, with a broad upholstered seat, and with either straight square legs, or bandy ones, much carved about the knees, and with the ball-and-claw foot, you may safely say, "Ah, Chippendale," and nobody will snub you. As a matter of fact, it is not difficult to recognize Chippendale furniture. His style is strongly marked. But wait until you come to the hair-splitting differences between Hepplewhite and Sheraton—which come right now.

ANTIQUES

HEPPLEWHITE ought really to be preceded by Adam, who in 1760 was the first to design furniture in the "classic" manner. His designs took London by storm and for a long time old Chip's bandy legs and ornate carving were in the shade. You remember that many of Adam's designs were executed in Hepplewhite's shop. Well, all I ask you to do in passing is to give Adam credit for the inspiration he undoubtedly gave to both Hepplewhite and Sheraton. We do not want so much to distinguish between Adam and Hepplewhite as we do between Hepplewhite and Sheraton. Both of these men were working at the same time along the same lines for supremacy, and it is between these two that most of the confusion exists. However, they did differ radically on some points, and we must make those clear.

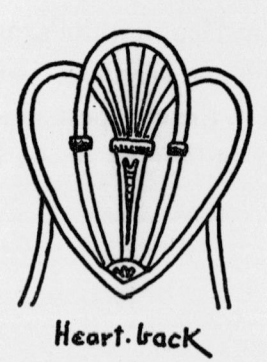

Shield-back

Heart-back

HEPPLEWHITE'S BACKS—The one outstanding distinguishing feature of Hepplewhite's chairs is the shield-shaped back. He got the idea from Adam, but he developed it so beautifully and gracefully after designs of his own that it became distinctly his. He was a lover of curves, differing in that from both Adam and Sheraton.

SHIELD BACK—Broadly speaking, all of his backs are curved, either in the shield or heart or loop shape. They are held up clear from the chair seat on short uprights, almost as if on exhibition. As a matter of fact, that was Hepplewhite's idea. He sacrificed strength for beauty, lightness, and grace, and some of his furniture was fragile to a degree.

HEART BACK—Within his shields and curves Hepplewhite employed various decorative carvings of his own, the three plumes of the Prince of Wales, interlacing hearts, wheat ears, carved drapery, the bellflower, etc. While he also used inlay extensively, he was much more fond of painting delicate and classic designs upon his finer pieces. The wood was usually mahogany or satin-wood. These are perhaps the most graceful and elegant appearing chairs ever made. But they are not the kind you sit down upon—or watch anyone else sit down upon—with any degree of pleasure.

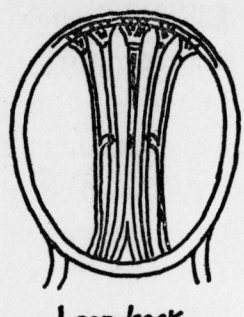

Loop-back

Hepplewhite's seats were ordinarily square or else slightly rounded in front and covered with upholstery. His legs were *invariably* straight, slender, and tapering, with or without the little spade foot. His chairs are lovely but lacking in a certain sincerity so apparent in Chippendale. I will tell you more about Hepplewhite under "H."

SHERATON published *his* book of designs in 1791, hot after Hepplewhite's of 1789. In the meantime, old Chippendale had laid him down to rest, leaving these two to fight it out alone. It was a battle royal. A case of snatch-as-snatch-can, each borrowing designs from the other until, in some instances, their work is identical. Sheraton's genius for proportion, his unfailing good taste and sensitiveness in decoration, however, show him to be unquestionably the greater man of the two. In fact, it is hard to imagine any one improving, either in practical soundness or in beauty, on Sheraton's designs for furniture. Here we have chairs as graceful as Hepplewhite's, as correct as Adam's, and as sound as Chippendale's. No wonder we see them everywhere, in homes and public places, in museum pieces and in the cheapest kind of reproduction. One sometimes wonders what would be left to sit on if we were suddenly deprived of all Sheraton's chairs.

Sheraton Backs

SHERATON'S BACKS—Sheraton's chairs were very like Hepplewhite's in general appearance: light, graceful, with square seats and straight legs, but they differed radically in the backs. While Hepplewhite's were curved Sheraton's were almost invariably rectangular. Often the top rail was clean cut and straight across, sometimes it was gently curved, and sometimes it was raised a bit in the centre. There was a straight rail at the bottom extending across the back a few inches above the seat. Thus he had a square frame in which to display his designs. These were numerous arrangements of delicate open-work panels or fretwork or spindles, sometimes occupying only the centre of the frame or extending clear across it. This fine work was often done in satin-wood, highly finished, decorated with the most exquisite inlay. When you add to this airy background a broad, generous seat, slightly rounded in front and completely covered in rich brocade the result is a chair of great elegance. Everything about these chairs was fine, classic in purity of line, perfect in refinement of decoration and yet they were warm and human in appeal, full of repose and strength. . . .

Sheraton backs are more extensively used in modern adaptations than those of any other maker. They are turned out of our factories by the thousands. You see them in hotels and dining cars, in clubs and restaurants. Those delicate, strong, correct backs, the humble offspring of the early aristocrats. Small wonder we should want to recognize them.

Practically every chair you see with a straight back and straight legs, having that lower back rail just above the seat, is Sheraton in inspiration.

Another point of difference between Hepplewhite and Sheraton chairs is in the legs. While Sheraton often used Hepplewhite's slender tapering legs he also used the round ones, which Hepplewhite never did. The typical Sheraton leg is round and reeded, tapering to the floor in a little plain turning. Sometimes these ended in a small turned ball.

Sheraton's work is sincere. He did not hesitate to make use of the designs of Adam or Hepplewhite or to improve and beautify them according to his need, but what he got from them or from any other source is lost in the vast output of his own facile and correct imagination. Sheraton is the most appealing figure in the history of furniture making. You will hear more about him under "S."

That finishes the "Big Four" so far as their chairs are concerned. We must now come back to America and see what is happening over here.

Of course, we were doing much importing and copying of the designs mentioned above, but we were also doing a good deal of our own. There was one man at least working in New York between the years 1800 and 1850 who turned out furniture in every way comparable with the best that England could produce. His name was DUNCAN PHYFE, and I will tell you about him under "P." He worked very much under the influence of both Adam and Sheraton, but he, too, was master enough to put something into his adaptations that resulted in a style entirely his own.

PHYFE'S BACKS—Broadly speaking, Phyfe's backs followed Sheraton's rectangular form (Phyfe was called the "American Sheraton") with the lower rail raised in the same way a few inches from the seat; but within the frame he worked out designs peculiarly his own, the most interesting and distinguished being the well-known "lyre back." Phyfe worked this lyre, sometimes with delicate brass rods for strings, on everything, but nowhere to better advantage than on chair backs.

Lyre-Back

MEDALLION BACK—He also used one cross-wise slat rather wide in the middle which was called a medallion back. Quite distinctive. And he differed, too, from Sheraton in that his uprights instead of being vertical swept down from the top rail in one long gentle curve, ending in a little curl-over that ran down the legs in a concave curve to the floor. Phyfe loved those unbroken long curves, often accentuating them with parallel rows of delicate reeding.

Phyfe worked in mahogany and his carving was exceedingly fine but entirely different from Chippendale's, being classic and Adam-like in feeling. His work deteriorated after 1820 under the Empire influence—he himself bitterly called Empire furniture "butcher furniture"—but his early work was well-nigh perfect in design and workmanship. America may well take pride in her greatest cabinet maker.

There, so far as we are able, are the chairs. It is a hard subject, by far the most important and interesting in the study of furniture, and, of course, we have no more than touched it here, but if you will study these outlines, especially the backs (I fear I have rather harped on backs), much of the first difficulty will be out of the way, and you can tackle each type in greater detail.

But do not become too fixed in your ideas about chairs. Do not, for instance, declare up and down that every Lyre-back chair is Phyfe's. You may safely say that it is one of his characteristic backs, and other details being equally characteristic, that such a chair is Phyfe's—at least in inspiration. Remember that chairs, like human beings, are individuals with family traits more or less obscured by interbreeding. Very few are pure aristocrats without a flaw. The bar sinister is usually lurking somewhere. The best we can do is to look for well-bred members of the old stock, and to recognize their good points when we see them.

CHESTS are probably the oldest form of furniture—and the simplest. While he was still content to sleep and eat on the ground, the cave man undoubtedly had some little cache where he hid his favourite stone ax. Then he put it in an animal skin so that he could carry it about, and then he made a box. Then he put a lock on the box, and locked boxes have been with us ever since.

Probably every Pilgrim who came over in the *Mayflower* had a chest, and after prayers were said these were the first things carried ashore, and where a man's chest stood, there was his home. The earliest chest had no drawers—just a crude box of oak or pine, more or less decorated with carving or mouldings, and with a hinged lid. It was used to sit on and lie on and work on, and contained the good wife's spun linen, the homespun garments, and bedding. After a few years the housewife got tired of digging to the bottom for everything she wanted and chests appeared with one long drawer below. Then with two drawers. Then chests were placed on a frame to save bending over.

While they were used constantly for many years afterward by those who already had them, low chests were not made to any extent after 1720. Up to that time they had been made everywhere all through the Colonies, the wood, workmanship, and design varying with the locality. They are a delightful study, the crude carving and painting on some of them being most amusing. We will mention only two familiar types, both carved and coming from New England.

CONNECTICUT CHEST—The best known and most easily recognized early chest. Made in the Connecticut valley from 1675 to 1700. The top, back, and bottoms are pine, the rest oak. They usually have two drawers. Three panels in front, the outer ones carved in the tulip design, and the centre with the wide-awake aster or sunflower. Turned "drop" ornaments on the stiles, and funny little egg-shaped pieces (perhaps the forerunner of the Connecticut Nutmeg!) appear on all of them.

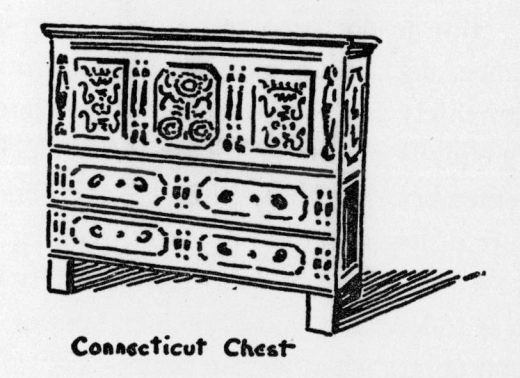

Connecticut Chest

ANTIQUES

HADLEY CHEST—Perhaps the most delightful chest is one found around Hadley, Mass. It usually had the initials of the owner carved in the centre one of the three front panels, and there were one or two drawers beneath. The entire front of the chest was covered with incised carving, usually in the tulip design, but the rest was plain. The carving was often stained with red, mulberry, and black. These chests are supposed to have been made about 1700 by a man named Hadley, from whom the town and the chest get their name.

Hadley Chest

Carved chests with three drawers are seldom found, but plain chests or those decorated with moulding often had three or even four drawers. They became, in fact, not chests *with* drawers, but chests *of* drawers.

TALL-BOY—About 1700 the chest of drawers was set up on a frame with six stout turned legs, four in front and two behind, and called a "tall-boy." The earliest type of a tall-boy was made in walnut (mahogany had not come in yet even in England) and was straight across the top. Dressing tables to go with them were made with four instead of six legs. . . . About 1720 the six turned legs gave way to four Dutch bandy or cabriole ones with two little acorns in front to show where the other two legs had been. These tall-boys were still straight across the top and were made in pine, in maple, either curly or plain, and sometimes in cherry, as well as in walnut. Very often the early pieces were painted, especially the simple pine and cherry ones.

This familiar and popular type of Tall-boy is eagerly sought by collectors, and occasionally may still be found in perfect condition.

Tall-boy 1700

HIGH-BOY—By 1740 we find the high "broken-arch" top that fifteen years later, when mahogany had become the fashionable wood, was so often beautifully carved with shells and scrolls and twisted torch flames. This type of handsome mahogany tall- (or high-) boy was particularly well made in Philadelphia by a Quaker cabinet maker named William Savery who lived from 1722 to 1787. He was evidently a close student of his great contemporary across the water, for he made fine use of mahogany, carving it superbly in the manner of Chippendale. . . .

LOW-BOY—All the time, of course, the little low-boys went through the same changes in treatment as their big brothers did. They were used as dressing tables with a mirror above them.

CHEST-ON-CHEST—About the same time the tall chest was set up on a frame two chests were sometimes placed one on top of the other, forming a large and commodious piece of furniture. It followed along with the tall-boy, changing as it did with the times. It was particularly handsome in Chippendale's time when it was often made with the fine block front and broken arch. High-boys and low-boys were never made with straight legs. In fact, after straight legs came in with Adam and Hepplewhite in 1770 high-boys and low-boys were no longer made at all. But the chest-on-chest survived, more beautiful than ever, severely rectangular in line, highly finished and inlaid, and with plain bracket feet.

Tall-boy 1740

Low-Boy 1740

Chest on Chest 1700

ANTIQUES

CUPBOARDS were the most pretentious pieces of furniture in the homes of the early settlers. In the simple homes—and those are the ones we like the most—they were made of native pine with narrow open shelves on which the pewter was arranged, and with a closet below for foodstuffs. These were called "dressers." But the man of property imported his cupboard from England or Holland—a massive affair, much carved, and decorated with moulding like the chests of the same period. There were many types of this heavy cupboard, but we will look at one, the typical

Presse Cupboard

PRESS CUPBOARD—A massive oak, two-tiered cupboard with no open shelves. Both the upper and lower sections had doors, and there were shelves or sometimes drawers in the lower section. They were elaborately carved and decorated with turnings. Very often there were thick turned posts at either end of the upper part and the cupboard cut away at an angle beneath them, an attempt at lightness that didn't get very far . . . The housewife always kept a bright piece of velvet or damask or some such thing on top on which to set her finest glass or silver, so it is quite all right to display your glass or lustre that way if you like. They put things on the straight-topped tall-boys too, on little steps made for just that purpose.

Those were clumsy cupboards, and if we had been living then how eagerly we would have welcomed the dainty corner cupboard that came in about 1710!

Many of these lovely corner cupboards, especially in pine, are still to be found in old houses. When you see one, take it out bodily—or buy the house—for there is no more lovely expression of Colonial days than this.

CORNER CUPBOARDS—These got back to the open-shelf idea, and at first were built solid into a corner of the room to match the pine panelling. . . . Then they were made detachable, of pine or maple or cherry, usually with doors only on the lower cupboard part. . . . These cupboards were made primarily to display the finest tablewear. And how perfectly they did it! The narrow shelves were daintily curved and scalloped with little projections to accommodate the bigger pieces, such as bowls and pitchers, and the top often filled in with a beautiful carving cut from the solid wood in the form of a sunburst or shell. Sometimes these exquisite shell tops were painted sky-blue, which gave the cupboard a positively celestial appearance; little shrines for the dearest household gods. Later ones were made with glass doors. Such a cupboard was called a "beaufett" after the French *beau-fait*, meaning beautifully made—a perfect name for these charming cupboards. The Colonists seemed to love cupboards and closets—who doesn't? They built them in everywhere; under the stairs, beside the fireplace, behind sliding panels; and it is these unexpected and naïve cubbyholes with their funny little doors and "H" hinges that add so much to the charm of an old house.

KAS or KASSE (case)—This odd cupboard came from around Dutch New York and Pennsylvania. A huge high wardrobe with big doors, and shelves inside for linen. It was often gaily carved and painted as the Dutch chests were. It is really more of a wardrobe or *armoire* than cupboard.

Corner Cupboard

Painted Kas

ANTIQUES

CLOCKS is another fascinating subject, and a big one, too. So far, the "C"s have all the best of it. I haven't the slightest idea what makes a clock go, and I am sure I could live in a clockless world for seven thousand years without ever trying to make one. The shadow on the hills or the swift trickle of sand in the hour glass would be enough for me. Why worry about the seconds as they fly into eternity? If man could make a clock that would catch a few I could understand his ceaseless and passionate interest in making clocks. However, clocks are charming objects even if they can do no more with time than tell it.

Although clocks had been made for centuries they were still a luxury at the time of the Colonies. The early settlers contented themselves with a glance at the sun which began and ended their day. The clocks they had were set upon a shelf against the wall and the long pendulum swung back and forth in a slit in the shelf. These were called "Wag-at-the-wall" clocks. It was probably to protect the pendulum that the first tall clock cases were made.

Tall Clock 1722

Wall Clock

TALL CLOCKS came into use about 1700. The earliest American tall clock still in existence was made by Bagnell in Boston. It is in a pine case and inside the door is written: "This clock put up Jan. 10, 1722," so you see, Massachusetts had an early start in the clock business, and it was not long before a family came along that rooted it to the soil for ever. These were the Willards—a family of twelve, of whom at least five made clocks. . . . The greatest of these, Simon, was born in 1753 and he made clocks steadily all through the Revolution and up to 1848, when he died, leaving, besides all the clocks, eleven children. When you realize that all his brothers were doing equally magnificently, and their sons after them, it isn't surprising that you come across an occasional "Willard clock." . . . Simon, as was the custom of that time, used to peddle his clocks around the country in a wagon. Two or three times a year he would start out, going from village to village, selling his clocks to the local casemakers, which explains why there is such variety in the cases, some of them simple pine or maple or cherry, others in mahogany elaborately and beautifully carved. Of course, all of these clocks were "Willard" clocks.

BANJO CLOCKS—In 1802 Simon Willard invented the charming "Banjo" clock which he patented, and its success was so great that he practically gave up making tall clocks except to special order. He also secured many commissions for tower and gallery clocks, and once while he was installing one in the United States Senate he met President Jefferson, who became his friend. He put clocks in the University of Virginia, and gave four to Harvard which he kept in order all his life. . . . He died in his ninety-fourth year, a fine old granddaddy of the "Grandfather" clock. I wonder if it was one of his that "stopped, short, never to go again, when the old man died"? I do not believe so. It would not have pleased the proud old fellow. His clocks knew better than to stop.

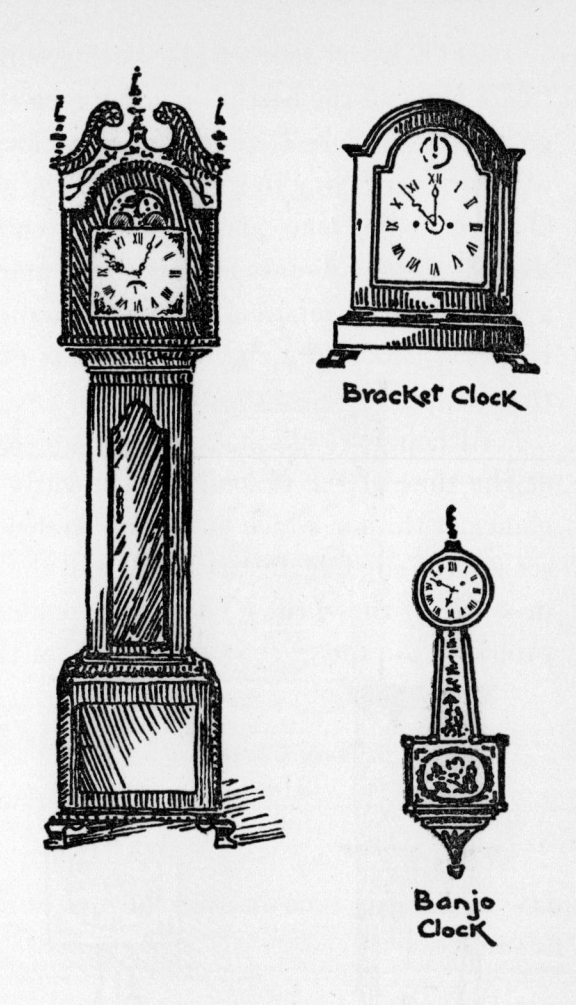

Bracket Clock

Banjo Clock

In the meanwhile Connecticut was getting all worked up about the clock business in Massachusetts, and in 1792, when Simon Willard was in his prime, a young man named Eli Terry began making clocks in Watertown, Connecticut. Terry was a great mechanical genius, and while his clocks may not be as fine as Willard's, he must be given credit for turning a journeyman's trade into a great industry. He, like Willard, made brass clock works, and every so often he tied a dozen or more to his saddle and peddled them on horseback. This clock peddling was soon too slow for Terry. He took in two assistants, Seth

ANTIQUES

Thomas and Silas Hoadley (who afterward made clocks of their own), introduced water power into his plant, and in 1807 took on a contract for four thousand clocks to be delivered in three years. People thought he was mad, but he did it, and from that time on his business was the biggest in the country. In 1814 he perfected a shelf clock that put the old tall case out of the running for ever.

TERRY CLOCK—The popular pillar-and-scroll short-case clock. It has a rectangular mahogany case about twenty-one inches high, with small bracket feet, and the top cut in a graceful scroll. At the sides are delicate round pillars tapering at the top and ending in a turned cap. The wooden face is painted and so is the glass door. . . . These clocks were immensely popular. Thomas paid Terry one thousand dollars for the right to make them and they both put them out by the hundreds. . . . These clocks are easy to find. Usually either Terry's or Thomas's printed instructions are still pasted in the back. Of course, the Terry clock is the more desirable.

Terry Clock 1814

Thus Eli Terry set going the millions of Connecticut timepieces that to-day are keeping time all over the face of the earth. He was the first American manufacturer to make a fortune out of "quantity production."

A word about wooden works. It is supposed by some of us that wooden works are older than metal ones, perhaps because they look so much more clumsy and crude. On the contrary, brass works are as old as or older than wooden ones, which were used only for convenience or for economy. Wooden clocks were always inferior because of the works being affected by the atmosphere, warping so that they jammed, and so on.

D

The party sat silent for a moment while Alice thought over all she could remember about ravens and writing desks—which wasn't much.
—LEWIS CARROLL: "Alice in Wonderland."

DESKS were very simple things in Colonial times, just a pine or oak box with a slant top. While some of them were crude and plain, they were more often than not much decorated with carving or with mouldings, as would be natural with so small and personal a piece of furniture. Writing materials and paper were kept in them, and also that most precious of all Pilgrim possessions—the Bible. They were made of a size to hold the big book, and were called Bible boxes. After a time they were made larger and set up on a turned frame like the chests, and the lid, instead of opening away from the writer toward the wall, was made to drop toward him. Pigeonholes were added. This was the beginning of the slant-top or drop-front desk. William Penn's desk was one of this type.

DROP-FRONT DESK—By 1710 the space below the desk box had been filled up with drawers, the drop-down lid, which rested on two little wooden "pull" supports when open, closed on the slant. Behind the lid was a simple arrangement of small drawers and pigeon-holes. This familiar slant-top desk was the foundation of every desk that has come since and is with us in much the same form to-day. They were made all through the 1700's in pine and maple and cherry, some of them crude, some painted. Some of the later mahogany ones were beautifully carved, and the maple ones inlaid with bird's-eye veneer and ebony. . . . The late maple ones usually have an ebony or mahogany star inlaid in the centre of the lid, and little stars appear on the tiny drawers inside. . . . Sheraton says, in his book of designs

Slant-top Desk

35

Drop Front Desk

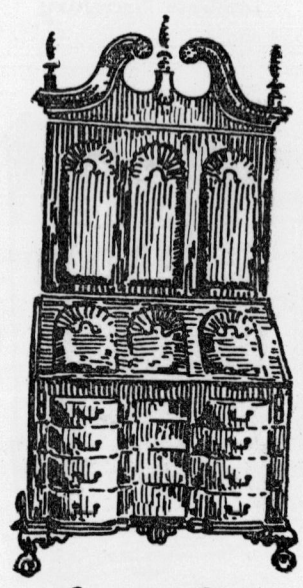

Secretary Desk

published in 1792, "These common desks with drawers made under them are nearly obsolete in London." So it is probable that most of the old ones you see (and they are not hard to find) were made not later than 1800.

SECRETARY DESK—About 1730 a bookcase was set on top of the drop-front desk. This soon developed into the handsome type of desk called the "secretary," a most beautiful and important piece of furniture. Except for simple ones made in the country of pine and more rarely of maple, the finest of these were walnut, and later on mahogany. By 1770, when Chippendale's fine designs were everywhere, this type of secretary had reached its highest development and was a tall, handsome piece of furniture with a broken-arch top and the drawer fronts blocked or bowed from the solid mahogany, like the high-boys and chest-on-chests. The doors were solid panels of wood or looking-glass and the interior was finished with numerous and carefully fitted little drawers and pigeon-holes. . . . There were few banks or safe-deposit vaults in those days, so in nearly all of these important desks there were secret drawers for the safe keeping of valuable papers. These were usually concealed behind a little door in the middle of the interior. Behind that door were tiny drawers, and by taking out certain ones of these the whole nest of little drawers came out, revealing still tinier ones behind. These, in turn, slipped back, revealing others, until sometimes eight or ten were found, and as the first little door wouldn't open in the first place until you poked a certain secret spot, they were pretty well concealed. In fact, sometimes the remotest of them were unsuspected for years, and when at last discovered, were found to contain wills and such-like papers that changed the current of many lives. These secretaries also had little candle stands that slid out from between the desk and the bookcase, and in the wooden pulls that supported the lid there were little places for pens. All of these tiny drawers and compartments were carefully finished and fitted with the care and pride that workmen took in their work in those days. . . . There were, of course, fine slant-top desks similar to these but without the bookcase.

HEPPLEWHITE AND SHERATON SECRETARIES—When Hepplewhite and Sheraton came in, desks as well as all other furniture became lighter in design. The grand broken arch gave way to the simple horizontal top, glass was put in the doors, and light woods, much veneering, and inlays were used. Bird's-eye maple trimmed with mahogany veneer and outlined in ebony inlay was a favourite combination in this country, and exquisite it was, too. . . . We will not go into the slight differences between Hepplewhite's and Sheraton's designs for secretaries except to say that those called Sheraton were, perhaps, daintier because of the delicate "tambour" sliding doors that were used to conceal the pigeon-holes. . . . Washington had such a tambour desk. His will reads "my bureau (or as cabinet makers call it, tambour secretary)." . . . The "tambour" was made of tiny strips of wood mounted on cloth so that it was flexible and would roll. The roll-top office desk of to-day is based on the same idea. . . . I know

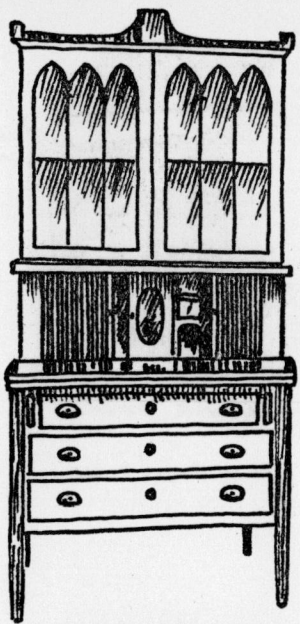

Tambour Secretary

Bookcase

ANTIQUES

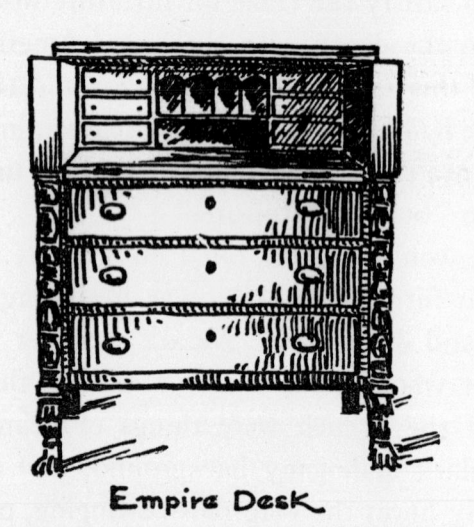

of one such tambour secretary that is exquisite beyond words. It is tiny, not more than six feet high!—and it has *thirty-six* secret drawers of sandalwood, each with a tiny ivory knob concealed under the moulding at the top and in the desk part.

Knee-hole Desk

BOOKCASES—These great pieces were built into or stood against the wall, usually in three sections, the desk part being in the centre section. Hepplewhite's designs for these were masterpieces, the huge things being positively graceful. They cannot be called desks, however, although they contain a desk.

KNEE-HOLE DESKS—Of course, all the while the tall secretaries were being made there were low desks, too. There was, for instance, the handsome flat-topped desk with the blocked front, the middle block receded to give place for the knees. They came in about 1760. They are called "Knee-hole" desks and were made of mahogany splendidly carved. Then there were the little "ladies' writing tables" elaborately inlaid and having the appearance when closed of a small flat-topped table. Sometimes they had a few drawers on top behind a dainty tambour.

Empire Desk

EMPIRE DESKS—Under the influence of the Empire, desks changed with the rest of the furniture. They became massive and square with heavy posts, carved with pineapple and acanthus design up the sides, like bureaus. The lid folded back on top like the lid of a piano or dropped down straight like the early Dutch desk.

E

Westward the course of empire takes its way.
—BISHOP BERKELEY: "On the Prospect of Planting Arts and Learning in America."

EMPIRE is the last of the so-called "period" styles in furniture, and it covers a multitude of sins. It is easy to remember that Empire means Emperor, that Emperor means Napoleon, and that this was Napoleon's idea of furniture. It expressed his personality perfectly. It was revolutionary, strong, coarse, and ornamented with much brass. Everything that was light and artistic had been kicked into the rubbish heap as the aristocracy had been, and we have square lines, heavy columns, and much carving of Egyptian sphinxes, lions' claws, and cornucopias. But, alas, such was the power of Napoleon's personality that he imposed his pretentious bombastic furniture upon the whole world. England meekly followed the "Dictator" to such an extent that even Sheraton was forced to satisfy the craze for furniture in the "French taste" until he descended into the depth with the rest. America, with her hatred for anything British—all this happened between 1793 and 1830 —also looked to France. Fortunately we had Duncan Phyfe, whose restraining influence kept us for years from falling into the utter ugliness of Europe, until he, too, in his old age, succumbed to the "butcher furniture."

Those who admire Empire furniture won't like this, but I do not care. I think its advent just at the time when furniture making was beginning to flower into perfection was devastating and disastrous. We are not over the effects of it yet. Of course, it was not wholly bad. No one and no thing ever is. The hand-wrought brasses of the French were things of beauty, especially when mounted against the dark mahogany background, and the Empire brought back at least two lovely lines: the long down-swinging, out-curving line of the table and chair legs (copied from the Roman curule chair and used earlier by Adam) and the Greek curl-over cornucopia line so much in fashion on the ends of sofas. But, taken as a whole, to my mind there is little beauty in old Nap's ideas of furniture.

ANTIQUES

AMERICAN EMPIRE—And yet I remember a little girl who, on a visit, used to love to slip through a high, wide-panelled door into a cool dim room, alone. There was a black carpet on the floor with small square gardens of roses all over it. Against the wall was a long "slippety-slide" horsehair sofa with terrifying lions' claws, and hard round cushions that tucked in tight under the curve of the arms. A wonderful lamp, with a Roman soldier holding aloft a snowy round globe dripping with sparkling icicles, stood on a square table with more lions' claws beneath. A tall mirror in a wide gilt frame with golden acorns hanging from the top reflected her courtly bows and bobbing pigtails, and if she touched ever so lightly the yellowed ivory of the piano keys, a plaintive tinkling sound came trembling from behind a red silk music rack into the quiet room. . . . All this, they tell me, was Empire. Perhaps it was. Perhaps the lions and the sphinxes were there, but they were snoozing, for (or so it seems to me) the Emperor Napoleon was very, very far away.

Pineapple Top

F

"Caveat emptor"

FAKES and REPRODUCTIONS are two ogres that lurk beside the path of the amateur collector, ready to pounce out and scare him almost to death. They are there, no possible doubt about that, and they will certainly get you if you don't watch out. But like many another ogre, they are not such bad fellows after you know them. The only trouble is they are rather hard to get acquainted with without being bitten first, for like the boy in the fairy tale, you have to go through the dark woods and learn to know them all by yourself.

Most people start out with one of two opinions: either that reproductions are just as good as originals, or that they are all a hideous crime against the sanctity of the true antique. I have had both phases of the fever and have come through with the opinion that neither of them is sound. It is obvious that the first one is wrong. No reproduction, no matter how carefully and honestly it is made, can ever be as good as an original. It will lack the indefinite but precious something that only Time can give. The very originals themselves must have lacked it when they came fresh from the hands of their makers, and they have a beauty now that we might have looked for then in vain. There is no question about this being true, and it is only the most stubborn and short-sighted of collectors who will buy reproductions when originals are to be had.

On the other hand, we all admit that there are not enough originals to go around, even among people who have the money to pay for them, and it does seem reasonable to fill out the chinks with good reproductions rather than go without the pieces entirely. It is really the only way the average collector can hope to have a harmonious whole. In fact, there are thousands of simple every-day homes where originals are out of reach, and these can be most delightfully furnished entirely in reproductions. I know more than one such home where the full flavour of the old Colonial days has been captured

ANTIQUES

to an astonishing degree with nothing but reproductions—and at a minimum of expense. This seems to be a consummation devoutly to be wished. It may smack, at first, of "standardization," but it is the first step toward a popular desire for furniture of our own American types—a much more valuable thing than an occasional exclusive collection of originals.

But—and it is a large but, too—do not buy reproductions if the originals are to be had and are within your means. You will regret it if you do. Everyone who can should do his utmost to capture these fine old pieces while he may, and, once he is lucky enough to own them, take the best possible care of them. It is not only a pleasure but a duty to preserve them. Too often we see beautiful pieces, that have been bought by people with more money than brains, falling apart from neglect—a really heart-breaking sight.

So far we have been talking about reproductions. Now for a word on fakes. There is a vast gulf fixed between fakes and reproductions. The reproduction is honest and the fake is not. It is meant to be sold as genuine and for that reason is much more carefully made and comes much nearer to looking like the real thing. The merest tyro can tell a reproduction at a glance. It often takes an expert, with years of experience behind him, to detect a fake. One would argue from this that fakes are better to own than reproductions, and the kind of people Barnum had in mind undoubtedly think so. They like to be fooled, and it is they who keep the fake makers busy all over the world. As a matter of fact, a fake is utterly worthless from any point of view because it isn't real. Nobody minds an honest *nouveau riche* reproduction, but a sham aristocrat is no good at any time.

It would be nice to know how to avoid fakes, but unfortunately it is extremely difficult to give practical advice about it. They are such clever fellows! There has been much serious matter written about how to examine furniture so as to avoid pitfalls, but, alas! as soon as these warnings are written the faker reads them and straightway makes his fake to cover the suspicious points. I remember once reading a splendid warning about wormholes: that artificial ones were made with bird shot that goes straight in, whereas the real ones were bent and twisted. At the end of the article was a little N. B.: "And now come wormholes bored by augers with lead shafts that bend!" The fakers had fixed *that* before the book got to press! Yes, indeed! For ways that are dark and tricks that are vain the heathen Chinee is a novice compared to the furniture faker. It is hopeless for the amateur to try to detect any but his rawest work. Half knowledge is worse than none at all, so the only safe thing the amateur can do is seek the advice of an expert he can trust—and then forgive him if he is wrong.

There are certain fakes that have recently been so well aired that everybody knows them. One is the antique maple twin beds. Of course, there were no such things or anything approaching them, and yet until recently hundreds of them were sold at top prices as "antiques." It takes a pretty bold dealer to try that now. As one of them confessed to me a few days ago, "I don't tell them no more it's antique. I tell them it is made off old vood." Well, that is something, and there is the possibility of its being true. At any rate, it is the only way one can have maple twin beds. And think of the maple "Constitution" mirrors that have been sold by the hundreds as old, when to all practical purposes old ones do not exist. There are a few, to be sure. The Metropolitan Museum is lucky enough to have one, but what about those we see in every wayside shop? Trust them not; they are fooling thee! These are only by way of obvious example.

Of course, any one, if he will take the time and trouble and can bear up under blows, can become fairly expert by continuously and carefully observing old furniture every chance he gets. That is the way the experts became experts, and there is no other royal road to knowledge of this kind. But if you are patient and honest with yourself the knowledge will come. Presently you will see things and hear voices, for I am perfectly certain, myself, that these old pieces that have lived for years with people, felt the touch of their hands, felt the weight of their tired bodies, listened to their endless talk, have caught something of the human quality that "gets across" to you. One friend of mine, an expert collector of old glass—perhaps the most difficult of all things to recognize—says that these things "speak" to her. And I believe her. I have had them speak to me. I do not know just how. Perhaps it is the *patine* which, when you have once learned to recognize it, can never be mistaken. Perhaps it is the look of individuality that old pieces have. At any rate, you will learn to know a genuine old piece the moment you lay eyes on it.

It is the other way around that the difficulty comes in; when you see a piece that looks very, very old, but that somehow does not convince you. You sniff and tap and peer and everything seems all right, but you listen in vain for the still small voice that whispers convincingly, "I am." Then is the time to look out, and if it is a piece of real importance hasten to your expert friend. And speaking of importance, do not be misled by the fact that the dealer is asking a big price for the piece. Remember that one of the most ancient ways of convincing people that they are buying the "real thing" is to make them pay a very real price for it.

But when you do have the good fortune to find a piece that speaks, that fairly pleads with you, take it. You may make a mistake, of course, but it is easier to get rid of a piece you do not want than to go through life with a gnawing regret. I know. I once, years ago, let go an exquisite Sheraton secretary with tambour doors. The memory of it stings to this day. One of the first principles of successful collecting is to know when and how to buy—quickly!

G

Chaste as the icicle that's curded by the frost from purest snow.
—SHAKESPEARE: "Coriolanus."

GLASS is a subject that we can only touch upon here, but it is so full of interest and fascination that it will be hard to boil it down. Speaking of boiling, that is the way glass was made—much clean sand, some lead and other things, according to recipes of different makers, were placed in a pot and subjected to terrific heat for from sixteen to thirty-six hours. As it melted, the impurities were skimmed off, just as we clear jelly, and on the care used in cleansing depended the quality and clearness of the glass. Thick, coarse, green glass, full of bubbles and "tear drops," is the result of careless cooking and poor material. When the stuff was properly boiled and cooled, the gatherer dipped off a bit and blew into it just as we blow a soap bubble. Someone else attached a piece of wood to the end of the bubble, the blower elongated a neck, someone snipped it from the end of the blow-pipe, and there was a blown bottle. Or the melted glass was poured into moulds, in two or three sections, and when these sections were set they were fused together as a whole—and there was a piece of "two-" or "three-mould" pressed glass. All glass making in the olden days (and for all I know even now) was based upon these two simple processes.

It is easy to see what fun it must be to make glass, to try and make it crystal clear, to add colour, to dally with delicate shapes; so it is no wonder that glass has been made since the beginning of history. There is no tomb in Egypt so old that it does not contain glass, and as glass resists decomposition better than almost any other substance, very old glass is often found in perfect condition. But we have no time to go into the astonishing perfection of early glass, especially that of Venice in the 14th and 15th centuries, or to babble about the stained-glass windows of old Europe. We must hasten on to glass in America, which in itself is a "bookful."

Those early Pilgrims, who were without so many things, had little glass. They drank from pewter or leather cups and ate from wooden trenchers. We

ANTIQUES

do hear that in Jamestown, as early as 1621, a glass factory was started to make glass beads for trade with the Indians. Whether these beads caused the massacre in 1622 we do not know, but anyhow the factory disappeared, and we hear no more of glass making until it was made in Salem in 1638, in New York in 1655, and in Pennsylvania in 1683. The first successful glass factory, however, was in New Jersey, where one Caspar Wistar opened it in 1739. This man made window glass, of which the country was greatly in need, as well as remarkably fine bowls, pitchers, bottles, and other forms, in both plain and coloured glass. He was the first man to make those glass balls that were used as covers for bowls and pitchers, ranging in size from a foot in diameter to tiny marbles to fit little pitchers, and to decorate them and other forms with whorls or wavy lines of colour on another colour. You have seen those green balls whorled with white. He made charming scent bottles and all sorts of lovely things of great interest to collectors, who call it "South Jersey" glass. Perhaps if the romantic and remarkable Stiegel had not loomed up in front of him we should hear more of our first great American glass maker. By the way, it is said that the early coarse, dark green pocket flasks and big rum bottles were blown by the workmen from scraps or leavings, and the careless, clumsy way they are made—which makes them so fascinating—would lead one to think that this is true, rather than that they were factory products.

"BARON" STIEGEL—The romantic and pathetic story of "Baron" Stiegel reads like a fairy tale. No figure in our early industrial history stands out more vividly than that of this German boy who landed in America in 1750. Romantic myths cluster about his name, and more than one fine book has been written about him, telling of his snow-white steeds, his various castles where cannon mounted on the roofs were fired at his approach, of his generosity and devotion to his adopted country (at one time his was the only foundry that furnished cannon balls to Washington), his reckless extravagance, his sudden collapse and ignominious death. He lies to-day in an unknown grave somewhere near the foundry that knew the glory of his prime. All we can say here is that he went to work in Jacob Huber's large iron foundry in Brickers ville, Pennsylvania, in 1751, and in 1752 married Huber's daughter, Elizabeth. By 1757 he had saved enough to buy out his father-in-law, promptly tore down the old furnace, and built a larger one which he called the "Elizabeth" furnace. In 1765 his business had prospered enormously, and he began experimenting in glass making. . . . What extravagances and follies, what visions of "Big Business" led to his undoing we can only guess, but we know that in 1774 his factory and foundries were sold for debt—and Stiegel's business career was over. Then at the age of forty-six—"a thin, bent old man"—he settled down to a quiet life in Brickersville, earning a scanty living by preaching and teaching until his proud and ambitious spirit flickered out in death in January, 1785. Be sure to remember, when you see Stiegel's beautiful glass, that he made it for only ten short years, and breathe a sigh of regret for what might have been if the stings of outrageous fortune had not broken his spirit at forty-six! But fascinating as Stiegel is as a man, we must get on to his yet more fascinating glass.

STIEGEL GLASS is famous for its beautiful colour, fine texture, characteristic forms, and charming decoration. There is something about it that is unmistakable, even to the tyro in glass, for although it has been much imitated, there is something about genuine Stiegel that "speaks." Stiegel made, of course, all manner of household things, but his smaller pieces—beautiful bottles, salts, sugar bowls, and cream pots—are perhaps most characteristic. Certainly they are the most eagerly sought and are the gems of any collection. The blue colour of many of these is especially lovely, and the shapes are delightfully crooked and delicate. He also made purple and amethyst, and, most rare of all, amber glass. . . . He made plain clear glass, beautifully etched and engraved—flip glasses, tumblers, etc.—but the most interesting of all his wares is the justly popular enamelled glass in German style. He imported workmen to do the painting of naïve scenes and flowers in clear bright colours on white glass. These lovely cups and mugs were much imitated. You will find similar ones with mottoes, "Remember Me," "Friendship's Offering," etc., painted in colours, but not so bright and good as his. While all these are early glass they are not apt to be Stiegel.

ANTIQUES

But you will have to study Stiegel for yourself, and fascinating it is, too, but do not be too hopeful of picking up genuine Stiegel glass—because you won't. The lucky ones got it long before you and I woke up!

Glass factories were flourishing at the beginning of the 1800's, as is evidenced by the number of the fragile pieces that have survived, to say nothing of the innumerable hip flasks that abound in every collection. Those were the days when everything—furniture, china, silver, and glass—was decorated with the "spread eagle" or Washington or some other emblem that expressed the high tide of political feeling then agitating the United States. Apparently, when anything or anybody stirred the people they rushed off and blew bottles—not a bad way to let off political steam at that! But we must leave the study of various glass to the expert and touch only upon the output of one factory—the much-discussed Sandwich.

SANDWICH GLASS is perhaps the most glib of all the phrases on the lips of the ubiquitous dealer. Anything and everything in the way of pressed glass is "Sandwich"—and let it go at that. As a matter of fact, it is often true, for the output of this factory was so great and covered so long a time that a lot of Sandwich still exists. The only trouble is, there is much of it you do not want—the coarse, cheap commercial stuff that the factory put out in its later years. Early Sandwich, however, is beautiful, interesting, and well worth collecting, although one prominent collector I know (the same one to whom glass "speaks") will not touch it. She says it is "too late"; but that, I think, is going a little too far. I am very fond of early Sandwich myself.

The Sandwich factory began business in Massachusetts on July 4, 1825, and continued its enormous output until 1885. Its main product was pressed glass, and the greater part of the candlesticks, glass lamps, sauce dishes, fruit plates, etc., that were on the broad pantry shelves of those days came from there. The Sandwich factory perfected the process of pressing glass into moulds so that every detail was clearly stamped, and as many of their early designs were as delicate as lace, the result was a lovely glass. Practically the whole outer surface of early Sandwich glass is covered with delicate detail of stippling and tracery, giving it a silvery gleaming appearance that is unmistakable. This type of Sandwich is well called "Lace Glass." In later years much of this design was omitted, the glass became coarse and was sold in cheap sets. We shall try to describe only the early typical Sandwich.

CUP PLATES—These delightful little articles are the joy of every collector of Sandwich, not only because of their charm but for their historic value as well. They were used as "coasters" on which to set the cup while the tea was cooling in the saucer, for in those days people drank from the saucer—which is really the proper way, as the Chinese will tell you.

Just as other glass makers blew political symbols into bottles, so the Sandwich people pressed them into these little plates. There were dozens of designs falling into various groups, and it is the capturing of these that so fascinates the collector.

Groups of designs are called by various names—the "Bunker Hill," "Eagle," "Ships," "Henry Clay," "Harrison," etc.—and some of the patterns are exceedingly rare. Those struck off in honour of President Harrison in 1840 show the log cabin that may be called the "trade-mark" of that canny old frontiersman. The log cabin and cider barrel appear on larger pieces, too, and that group of glass is called "Tippecanoe." Cup plates were made in yellow, blue, and opalescent, as well as in clear white glass, as were the little salt boats also so much sought; and so, of course, were the larger pieces in use at that time.

VICTORIAN SANDWICH—About 1870 Sandwich turned out great quantities of coarse opaque white glass in the forms of animals, setting hens, owls, ducks, cats, etc. They were used by various commercial houses to induce people to buy their goods before the days of the soap-wrapper premium package, etc., and very attractive containers they were, too. Some of them were made in a lovely light blue glass with fine glass eyes, and the rarer ones of these are liked by collectors who are not over-"highbrow." We have a little blue hen sitting on our breakfast eggs every morning.

This is just a taste of a fascinating subject that has been covered over and over again in many fine big books, for nothing is more intriguing when you once get started than the study and collecting of old glass.

Fluted Tumbler

Creamer

Cockatoo Tumbler

Barrel Tumbler

"Stiegel" 1770

Bottle

White Flint Glass

Cup-plate

Dolphin Candlestick

Setting Hen

Salt Cellar

"Sandwich" Pressed 1840 Glass

E.S.

H

The work of their hands has worn well, and the work of their brains has guided well the hands of other men.
—GEORGE ELIOT: "Adam Bede."

HEPPLEWHITE, you remember, was the third of the "Big Four," but while he ranks high in the group, to me he has always seemed a sort of middle man. He had not Chippendale's sense of proportion, Adam's unsullied inspiration, or Sheraton's fine feeling for designs and decoration. Everybody copied, of course, or got inspiration from some source, but in Hepplewhite's case the tail sometimes seems to wag the dog. His French furniture is so French as to be nothing else; he got many of his decorative ideas from Adam (whose furniture designs he executed) and some of his and Sheraton's pieces are identical. On the other hand, he published a big book of valuable designs—at least, such a book was published by his widow—and there are certain splendid details about his work that mark him unquestionably as a great master. While he worked a great deal in mahogany and did some delicate carving, he preferred light wood, decorating it with beautiful inlay or more often with painting in place of carving. He took Adam's straight lines and carried them along, using curves inside the straight frame wherever he could. Chippendale's forms and decorations were entirely in the discard by now. Gone were the fat bandy legs for slender straight ones. Gone the massive high-boy with the broken arch. Secretaries, chest-on-chests, bookcases, tables, all had straight clean lines and much delicate inlay for decoration.

Little is known of Hepplewhite's personal history except that he conducted his business in St. Gile's Parish, Cripplegate, and that he died in London in 1786. After his death the business was carried on by his wife under the name of A. Hepplewhite & Co. It was she who published his book in 1788 and again in 1789 and again in 1794. She must have been a remarkable woman to manage such a big business in those times, and there is a myth to the effect that Alice herself was Hepplewhite. I do not believe this, but I do believe that she had a lot to do with the delicate designing of much of his work. For one thing, Hepplewhite's designs are so varied in merit. Some of them are positively inspired and then again he sinks to mediocrity—and you may lay the blame for this unevenness where you will. Certainly the underlying spirit in Hepplewhite's work is one of lightness and grace, sometimes at the sacrifice of practicability.

What Hepplewhite did with the chairs and tables, etc., is discussed under those heads. As there is so little known about him personally, there is nothing more to say about him here—except to wonder how much of his popularity is due to the pleasure we find in those beautiful words "Hepplewhite of Cripplegate."

Hepplewhite Detail

HARDWARE is a hard subject—naturally! I can see it piled up, a perfect junk heap of old andirons, pot-hooks, tongs, cranes, Franklin stoves, cooking-pots, skewers, footwarmers, lanterns, hinges, and warming-pans, and as often happens in a junk heap, there are many treasures there. All we can do is pick out something here and there to bring the subject to your attention, hoping that you will follow it up in the books devoted to the subject.

The history of the iron industry in early Colonial days is much like that of glass. There were iron foundries here as early as 1640—the first iron kettle was cast in 1642—but they were not really successful until the middle of the 18th Century. By that time they were flourishing, especially in Pennsylvania. You remember that Stiegel went to work in Huber's big foundry in 1751. In the meantime, raw material and finished articles had been imported in the amazing sailing ships that were constantly unloading their cargoes on our shores. Some of us have the idea that the Colonies were an isolated wilderness where the people lived a sort of Robinson Crusoe existence, battering together the bare necessities of life in nature's workshop. That, largely speaking, was not true. They were nothing like as isolated as were the Western pioneers, later on when everything had to be carried in ox-carts over thousands of miles of desert. Shiploads of fine furniture and handsome materials came to the Colonies continuously and from the very start, and the standard of living among the better—or rather richer— people was astonishingly high. Look, for example, at the hardware alone on that famous list of things ordered by Judge Sewall in 1719 for his daughter, Judith, about to be married—a generous and sagacious list, if there ever was one: "a bell-metal skillett, a warming-pan, four pairs of brass-headed iron dogs, tongs, shovel and fender in the newest fashion (the fire to lie on the iron), a brass mortar, four pairs of brass candlesticks, four brass snuffers with stands, six small brass chafing dishes, two brass basting ladels, a pair of bellows with brass noses, a small hair broom, a dozen pewter porringers and a dozen good ivory hefted knives and forks." Not half bad for a girl supposed to be living the life of an aborigine on a stern and rock-bound coast.

ANTIQUES

Brass-headed Andirons

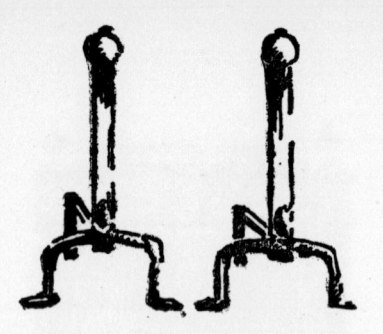

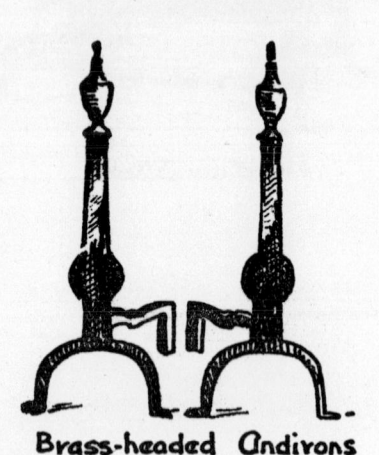

Hessians

ANDIRONS—The earliest fireplaces were extremely large. Wood was plentiful and the Colonists had the idea that the larger the log the warmer the room. The iron dogs for those fires were very large and heavy, made of hand-pounded iron. Above them swung the crane laden with simmering pots on pot-hooks of various lengths. The iron baking oven stood in front of the flames. The skewers, skillets, and ladles hung on the wall. Near by stood the warming-pan waiting for the comforting coals. In fact, upon the backs of the sturdy iron dogs rested all the blessings of the household. . . . But Judith Sewall's "brass-headed iron dogs" were daintier than these, and as houses grew larger, with more than one fireplace, handsome all-brass andirons came into use. As there were several pairs in every house and they were used continuously until stoves and furnaces came in, there are many to be found, lovelier in colour and lustre than the modern ones. The most common design was the "Colonial Pillar" topped by balls or turnings. The pointed "Steeple Top" is rarer and daintier. Fire tongs and shovels were made to match, but there was no poker with the earlier sets. It came in with the use of coal about 1750. Fenders of pierced brass or of wire, painted black, and topped with small brass balls, were used with the andirons. These things were largely imported from England, although all kinds of metal work was being done in America by 1750.

"HESSIANS"—In 1776 we had an andiron that was distinctly our own. It was cast in iron and painted to represent the hated "Hessian" allies of the British. Every household had a pair of these effigies down in the ashes and flames, and for years nothing pleased the victorious tobacco-smoking patriot more than to sit before his fire and cast indignities upon them. Sometimes these andirons are called "Minute Men." Perish the thought!

FRANKLIN STOVES—In 1745 Benjamin Franklin, exasperated by the smoky, draughty fireplaces, turned his inventive genius to the problem of saving fuel and at the same time getting more heat into the rooms. The result was the famous "Franklin stove." This was a cast-iron frame with a small flue and an open grate for wood, and later, coal. This was set into the fireplace and the surrounding space bricked up. This stove was immediately and immensely popular and was made in great numbers. Undoubtedly many of them were made in Stiegel's "Elizabeth" furnace. They are graceful in form, with brass knobs decorating the tops of the fenders and the frame. Do not confuse these with the English hob—a basket-like grate that sets inside the fireplace. The Franklin projects into the room. Franklin stoves are made to-day, and it is hard to tell the old ones from the new.

HINGES—The shapes of old hinges are fascinating and are often a good guide to the genuineness and character of a piece of furniture. Always look at the hinges, locks, and handles. These details are skilfully imitated to-day, but an old hinge is so wedded to the wood that it is pretty hard to fake. It is one of the things that "speak." I have an old pine chest with the in-

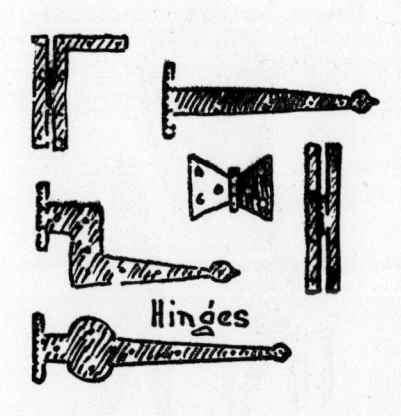

Franklin Stove

Hinges

ANTIQUES

Lion's Head

Spread Eagle

terlocked hinge—an early and simple form. While the wormholes in the wood, the secret drawer in the till, and the incrustation of old paint might not convince me, the hinges would. Many of the old chests have the long "strap" hinge, also good. There is the "Cock's head," a shorter branched hinge with leaves cut to resemble a cock's head, the familiar "H" or "HL" hinge so often seen on doors and cupboards, and, daintiest of all, the little "butterfly." These familiar hinges, and, of course, many others, were hand-wrought and used until about 1800. They are an interesting detail and well worth attention.

KNOCKERS—Door knockers were in use for centuries until the bell-pull and electric button came in, only yesterday. Then the dignified ornaments were unscrewed from the front door and either sold to the junk dealer or stowed away in the attic. Fortunately, time cannot mar nor rust destroy these beautiful brasses, so that many of them are coming to light again. I cannot agree with people who think that they should be replaced on doors, merely as ornaments. There is something jarring in seeing an electric button beside a knocker on a door. Why not use the knocker? It can be heard distinctly, it is a joy to use, and it never gets out of order. But then that is opposed to progress (whatever that may mean). Old knockers were made in many forms—the "Lion's Head" (English), "Spread Eagle" (guess where), "Hammer," and "Garland" types, but almost every old knocker has individuality of its own, which in turn gives character to the door.

HOOKED RUGS—The thrifty and inventive Colonial housewife made her own floor coverings. In the evening, when her heavy tasks were done, she sat before the fire cutting into strips old garments and scraps that she had saved, sewing them together, winding them into tight balls, and when enough of these balls were ready she made them into rugs. The simplest of these were braided and caught together with a heavy needle into strong round mats, or the strips were crocheted or knitted. These rugs are interesting and worthy of our attention, but the most fascinating and important of all are the justly popular "hooked rugs." They were made in New England and Canada—you never find them in the South—and I should like to take off my hat to the woman who made the first one. Probably she lived, about 1775, in some farmhouse in Vermont or Massachusetts, a lonely, ambitious, intelligent woman who, in the long winter evenings, hit upon this way of setting her fancy free. Perhaps she was inspired by the sampler that her little daughter's head was bent above, perhaps by the crewel work on some early counterpane, but however that may be, she "started something," and from that time on until well into the Victorian era, hooked rugs were made in every farmhouse in New England. I wonder what the first "drawed-in" rug looked like. Probably it was a picture of the farm with much of Father's old shirt in the bright red house. At any rate, these are supposed to be the oldest, and we find many of them still, with fences, barns, and everything. Then came the pictures of animals—the farm pets—"Fido" and the cat and the pony and the best-laying hen. Sometimes there were lions and tigers—wild flights of imagination—or ambitious copies of some bit of fine French brocade or chintz. Or perhaps it was just a well-remembered bunch of sweet posies from her own garden. Then there were "hit-and-miss" stripes showing less imagination but carefully done. In fact, one seldom finds a carelessly made hooked rug. They had pride, those women! These designs were the early ones, from 1800 to about 1830, but with the languishing sentimentality of Victorian days, the sturdy studies were put aside and we find "God Bless Our Home" and "Welcome" and "Good Luck" paving the floor. The colours in these were brighter than in the home-dyed wools and cottons of the earlier ones. Some of them are downright crude.

ANTIQUES

This is one case where crudeness means not the beginning but the decline of an art, so do not be misled into thinking that the ugly patterns are the oldest.

There was another type of hooked rug that we must speak of all by itself. It is the "marine" design—our clipper ships under full sail at sea. These beautiful rugs were made in the whaling ports of New England, supposedly for the cabins of ships. Many of the rugs with sailing ships that we see came from Newfoundland, where the design was and is popular, but both the work and the vessel are different from our own, so that it is not difficult to tell them apart. The New England clipper ship rugs are rare. The Newfoundland ones are not.

Hooked rugs were very simply made and it is pleasant to see that the art is being revived. You can buy the materials and instructions for making them in almost any "Art Department" to-day, but of course, our dyes are not as good, and we hurry them too much. However, better this than nothing. The best early rugs were made with stout hemp bagging for the back. This was tacked to a frame and the pattern drawn in charcoal upon it. Then the coloured worsteds or cotton rags or both were selected and "drawed" through the holes of the bagging from the back to the front with a coarse smooth hook. The loop of colour was pulled through as heavy or as light as desired, but evenly one loop in every square of the sacking. In some rugs you find the loop clipped off as in an Oriental rug, but I am inclined to believe that this was done only when the top surface was worn, to restore the bright colour from beneath. Some of these sheared rugs are marvels of evenness. In fact, a really fine early hooked rug is a marvel in every respect, in design, in colour, and in workmanship. It is incredible that we were blind to their beauty so long. Let us be thankful they are being rescued now and given a place of honour in the American home.

Hooked Rug

J

Some smack of age in you, some relish of the saltness of time.
—Shakespeare: "Henry IV."

JACOBEAN is a word that should be clearly understood by all of us who are interested in early American furniture because that is the kind of stuff that was brought over by the very earliest adventurers and pilgrims who came here. They had to bring it because that is what was being used in England when they came.

The Jacobeans were the followers of the Jameses and their sons, the Charleses, who had such a hectic time keeping on the throne of England from 1602 until the Dutch William and Mary came along in 1689. Right in the middle of the Jacobean period Oliver Cromwell took things in hand, and for eleven years, from 1649 to 1660, kept them all off the throne. The furniture made during those eleven years is called "Cromwellian" and expressed to a degree the cold Puritanical revulsion toward all ostentation.—Did you know, by the way, that Cromwell had taken passage and was actually on board ship for America when he was yanked off by the king? How Charles must have wished afterward that he had let him go!—After Cromwell himself went down, Jacobean furniture returned more or less to its former style and was called "Restoration."

Thus you see Jacobean furniture is divided into three groups, called "Early Jacobean," "Cromwellian," and "Restoration." The early type is what came here first, the heavy wainscot chairs and carved chests. Then came the simpler pieces severely ornamented with mouldings, followed shortly by much more carving added to the mouldings—spiral turnings, Spanish feet, Flemish scrolls, etc.

All this, however, happened between 1620 and 1689. Then with William and Mary the Dutch influence began to come in rapidly, so it is rather foolish for us in America to split hairs over the small amount of furniture that got to us before that time. For us, to all intents and purposes, at least for the amateur, it is just plain Jacobean.

ANTIQUES

Just a word about JAPANNING and LACQUER before we leave "J." There is some confusion between these two words, which are often used synonymously, and we will try to clear it up. You remember that by 1700 England was carrying on a lively trade with the Orient, and furniture decorated in lacquer in the "Chinese manner" became the rage. At first these handsome pieces were imported from the Orient, but soon the English and French cabinet makers were copying them, applying the Chinese decoration to every type of furniture. The craze for this lasted well through the century, and some of the superb pieces in red, black, or green lacquer, splendidly a-crawl with gold dragons and other Oriental symbols, are among the marvels of that time. They were heavily enamelled with coloured shellac, and the decoration was raised from the surface and painted with gold and colours. Furniture decorated in that manner at that time was called "japanned." Japanning became a fashionable pastime of the belles and beaux of the 18th Century who all had their boxes of colours and loved to dabble in the "arts."

But Hepplewhite introduced a new process of decorating furniture resulting in what he called "a very elegant fashion." It was the use of several coats of thin, clear, brilliant varnish on which he used painting in gold or colours. This process he called japanning, although it was not in the least like the earlier process by that name. However, Hepplewhite was right. The early furniture was lacquered, and his process was japanning. Hitchcock also japanned his stencilled chairs by protecting them with a thin coat of clear varnish. Stencilled tin is also japanned in the same manner. Any object treated with a coat of thin varnish such as the Japanese use on their bamboo, paper, etc., articles, is "japanned."

Jacobean Detail

L

Neither do men light a candle, and put it under a bushel, but on a candlestick; and it giveth light unto all that are in the house.
—St. Matthew, V, 15.

"L" BRINGS us to LAMPS and LIGHTING. The flaming pine knot was the first light used by the Pilgrims. There may have been a few candles on the *Mayflower* but candles were very scarce in the Colonies for many years. Tallow for making them was lacking, and those that were imported were too precious to burn except on state occasions. It was not until well along in the 1700's that housewives were able to dip or mould candles in any abundance. One word about making candles—one of the never-ending tasks of the busy housewife. She made them in two ways. The earliest way was to dip the wick into melted tallow, let it cool, dip again, until it reached candle size. This was a long-drawn-out and tiresome process, but it resulted in a lovely candle, and imitations of the old dipped candle are popular to-day. Sometimes the pungent, sweet-smelling oil of the bayberry was added to the tallow to offset its rancid smell, and these were burned on a holiday for good luck just as we use them now.

The second and later process was to pour the tallow into moulds, which was quicker, some moulds holding as many as thirty-six candles. Later still the candles were made by itinerant candle makers who could mould a winter's supply in a few days. What fun the visits of these "journeymen" candle makers and weavers and tinsmiths must have been! Surely they were jolly fellows, full of gossip, well fed (so that they shouldn't gossip too much in the next place), thrilling the household, from the children to the elders, with their tales of the open road.

There were candlesticks for all these candles, many of them in every house, much prized and constantly in use, so it is not surprising that we find them still.

ANTIQUES 64

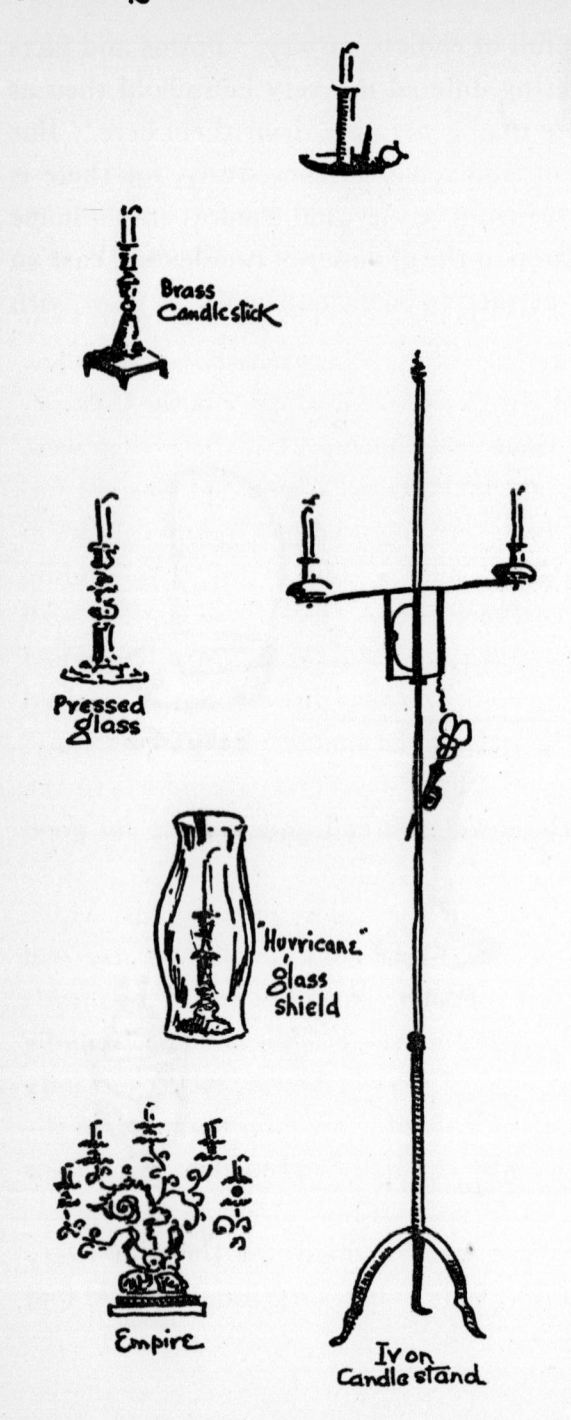

CANDLESTICKS—The early iron sticks were exceedingly plain, just a holder with a hook on the side so that the light might be hung over the chair back or wall. In 1696 tall iron tripods appeared with two branching candlesticks that could be slid up and down. Snuffers hung from them. Later candlestands were made of mahogany, beautifully carved (Chippendale's time), and a handsome silver candlestick, either single or with two or three branches, was set upon it—a lovely lighting arrangement. Fine brass sticks were placed on the mantelpiece in pairs, and there were charming low ones with broad bases for use in bedrooms. These "bed candles" were usually placed on a small table beneath the stairs, and one by one, as the household retired, the candles went twinkling up into the dark. It was often the custom of the host to light the candles from his own, handing them to his guests, as, with a courtly bow, he bade them good-night. . . . By 1775 candles were used abundantly and, in the homes of the rich, were hung from the ceiling in crystal chandeliers with sparkling prisms and crystal drops. The candle flames on these and on the single sticks were protected from the draught by tall glass globes, sometimes plain and sometimes etched. These were called "hurricane glasses." Perfect imitations of them are being made to-day. Pressed-glass candlesticks were used in great numbers after 1825, and these, too, were sometimes hung with the lovely drops and crystals. In the time of the Empire (1810 to 1840) candlesticks appeared in bronze heavily hung with crystal. They were followed by the ornate and fussy candelabra of many branches.

Both candlesticks and lamps are full of endless variety. Forms and facts overlap each other. Methods of lighting differed in every household then as they do to-day, and we can do no more than generalize about them here. But the subject of lighting is one that will well repay further study, for there is no one thing that goes so far toward bringing beauty and comfort into a home as proper lighting. A softly shaded lamp or the glimmer of candles will cast an enchantment over an otherwise not attractive room and make it glow with intimacy and charm.

BETTY LAMPS—The most familiar and appealing early Colonial lamp is the little "Betty," a tiny boat-shaped thing of iron or brass with a handle at one end and a short spout at the other from which protruded a twisted oil-soaked rag. Lamps similar to this had been carried by wise and otherwise virgins for countless centuries, and a job it must have been to keep them trimmed and burning! A chain with a ring was attached to the "Betty" lamp so that it could be hung on the wall. Whale oil and fat were burned in them before candles became plentiful. . . . Another very early and rare lamp was no more than a shallow square iron dish hung on a chain. It was filled with oil, and four wicks were laid in it at the corners. It must have been a dismal, smoky affair, which probably accounts for its being rarely found.

PEWTER LAMPS—After candles became more plentiful the little "Betty" flickered and went out forever. Then pewter lamps appeared with one or two tiny spouts for the wick. These were without shades and were little better than the Betty lamp, having to be picked at constantly to make them burn, but as they saved the everlasting candlemaking they were much used and are not difficult to find. One

Pressed Glass

Astral Lamp

variation of these lamps is delightfully called the "Sparking Lamp." It is a tiny thing, holding no more than a good spoonful of oil, and it is said that when a young man came a-wooing he had to leave when the oil in this lamp burned out. Perhaps the tininess of the flame compensated for the lack of fuel.

GLASS LAMPS—By 1800 lamps were in general use, and small blown-glass ones, similar to the pewter, with one or two tin tubes soldered to a pewter screw top, appeared. These simple lamps with heavy pressed-glass bases are not difficult to find and make charming bedroom lamps to-day.

EMPIRE LAMPS—The finer Empire lamps had imported coloured bowls attached to bronze pedestals and were decorated with prisms in true Empire fashion. This type of lamp became hopelessly elaborate during the Victorian period, with heavy marble bases, frosted globes, and countless prisms. The simpler lamps were often made in two colours, opaque white bases (like the Sandwich setting hens) with green or blue or opalescent bowls. We are all familiar with these naïve lamps.

KEROSENE LAMPS—In 1865 a flat wick was introduced and everybody had his lamp fixed over to accommodate the fine new flame. By this time an "improved lighting fluid" which we know as kerosene had taken the place of the animal and vegetable fats that had been used for centuries. Gas, too, which had been hanging fire since 1806, was now in general use. Electric lighting came with Edison's first public supply station in New York in 1881.

LUSTRE—the very word is glamorous. Probably the allure of lustre ware has done more to awaken interest in antiques than any other one thing. Long before we dreamed of furniture we were collecting lustre. I know I was. My very first "antique" was a little lustre cup, and it was a fake at that, a howling, shrieking, screaming fake, for, if you will believe me, it was a demi-tasse! But how I loved that little cup, and how I love it still. Every evening of my life I drink my coffee from it, and every time it touches my lip, like old King Thule, I weep and think of things long p-e-r-i-s-h-e-d. How young I was and how ignorant! How wonderful the days when everything at every wayside inn was real! I paid five dollars for that cup and carried it in my arms over many miles of rough motoring—my precious, precious antique. After all, nothing is more blissful than ignorance. If I thought that this little book would shatter it I would stop right here. But it won't. You will go right on making blissful mistakes, so I may as well continue. Lustre, remember, is not a kind of ware. It is a process applied to many makes of chinaware. It is a thin iridescent metallic solution into which the piece is dipped, or which is applied to it with a brush. Some pieces of lustre have mighty little lustre on them, just a dab here and there, others are completely covered inside and out, as in silver lustre pitchers, bowls, etc., that look almost like the metal itself. Usually it is about fifty-fifty, a wide band of lustre decoration encircling the piece as in the charming tea sets most commonly seen. Before we describe the several kinds of lustre let us say that it was always made in England, the mistaken idea that some of it was made here arising from the fact that the lustre intended for American trade was often "hall marked" with an American emblem. Lustre came from England; at first, from 1780 to 1800, in small lots, gradually increasing until by 1830 it was coming over in large quantities. Lustre was usually used on tea sets (the earliest cups are without handles), but there were beautiful bowls and pitchers as well, some of them decorated with historic scenes. One famous pitcher, made at the time of Washington's death, has "Washington in Glory" on one side and "America in Tears" on the other. Was this a magnanimous gesture on the part of the British maker, or had he just a shrewd eye for trade? Other harrowing scenes, "At Mother's

ANTIQUES

Grave," etc., are depicted, but these pieces are rare. What we usually see and adore are the little pink teacups, the little brown jugs, or the exquisite silver resist bowls.

PINK LUSTRE is the most popular of all lustre ware and the most easily found. It comes in charming little tea sets, often in "proof" condition, for our grandmothers used them carefully. Single cups and saucers are easily found, and the different designs are endless. My favourite is the tiny English cottage with its bucolic trees; or perhaps the strawberry pattern with trailing green vine and the berry made, you know, by pressing the thumb to the wet paint. The colour in these is a deep rose or pink under a thin wash of gold.

SUNDERLAND—All the English potteries turned out lustre, but the Sunderland potteries in Durham made it in great quantities. It is pink lustre characterized by the spotty marbled blotchiness that covers the whole piece. Some people collect nothing but Sunderland.

SILVER "RESIST"—This loveliest lustre was made by first painting or stencilling the pattern on to the piece to be decorated with some substance (perhaps glycerine) that would "resist" the metallic bath. This piece was then dipped into the silver (or copper) solution which covered all the surface except where the pattern had been stencilled. It was then washed off in water, which did not affect the lustre but which left the stencilled pattern clear. Usually the background of these pieces was white, but sometimes it was blue or canary-yellow, and anything lovelier than a silver "resist" pitcher with a yellow pattern cannot be imagined. Fine examples, however, are expensive and hard to find. . . . Perhaps we ought to say here that in applying a lustre design to a white or coloured ground exactly the opposite method was used. Then it was the lustre that was stencilled on.

COPPER LUSTRE—This brings us to the delightful brown jugs and mugs and pitchers. These run from two- or three-quart capacity to tinies. The more common ones were made of brown earthenware and had raised designs crudely modelled upon them. These were dipped into a thin copper solution and the outer surface completely covered. The prettier ones had bands or medallions of colour around them, blue, green, or yellow, with little bucolic scenes stencilled upon them, or tiny raised figures carefully painted in colours and picked out with dabs of lustre. Still finer pieces were made of white ware instead of brown, decorated in the same manner. Lustre pitchers are a life's passion with more than one sweetly mad collector, and I can think of no hobby more beatific unless, perhaps, it be collecting lustre bowls—which happens to be mine.

BENNINGTON POTTERY—We were going to keep discreetly away from china and pottery in this small volume, but since we have yielded to the impulse to talk about lustre we may as well say a word for Bennington pottery as well.

The interest that so many collectors have in Bennington pottery isn't because it is old—because it is not so very—but because it is quaint and unique. The products that we are chiefly interested in were made between 1847 and 1857, although the old pottery dates back to 1793, when a Connecticut potter of the name of John Norton moved to Bennington, Vermont, and opened a pottery there. The Norton family carried on the work without doing anything especially clever until 1846, when they formed a partnership with a man named Fenton, a person of skill and energy who at once began making Rockingham ware and the pottery we call Bennington. In 1849 the firm was reorganized again and called the United States Pottery, and they were lucky enough to engage the services of Daniel Greatbach, an Englishman with experience in the potteries abroad. In an effort to produce something like the Staffordshire figures he designed the Bennington figures that are so popular now, among them the famous "hound" pitcher which he had first originated in Jersey City and afterward produced at Bennington. That is why there is so much confusion between "Jersey" and "Bennington" hound pitchers. Those made in Bennington are much finer and are distinguished by the nicer modelling and the space between the hound's nose and the edge of the pitcher. It is a handsome and amusing pitcher, the hound forming the handle, and raised hunting scenes decorating the body of the piece. There were many other naïve and rather crude figures produced at Bennington, the familiar poodle with the basket in his mouth, the cow cream pitcher, the reposing stag, the coachman in the tall hat, and others too numerous to mention, and they were made in a variety of colours, mottled and variegated, but the most common was a rich, smooth, molasses-brown glaze of almost metallic lustre.

This, of course, only touches upon one small part of the Bennington output. The subject would well repay further study.

STAFFORDSHIRE—And we may as well say, too, while we are here, that the word "Staffordshire" that we hear so much, "Staffordshire figure," etc., it is not the name of any particular make of china, as we might well suppose. It is the name of a county in England where many different famous potteries are located, so that "Staffordshire" is a sort of blanket word which means nothing more than that the piece was made in that district. As all sorts of china and pottery, both good and bad, were produced there, it does not give one much clue to what one is buying to call it "Staffordshire."

China Dog

M

*"In vain sedate reflections we would make
When half our knowledge we must snatch, not take!"*
—Pope: "Moral Essays."

MIRRORS, or looking-glasses as they were called in the old days, are the most cold, impersonal, and interesting objects in the house. All things change except the surface of a mirror, which sees all changes. When you think of the happiness, the misery, the terror, the changes of fashion, and the miracles of science that have been reflected in their lidless, non-committal, ever-vigilant eyes without leaving one trace of their passing there, the mirror becomes not only interesting but awe-inspiring as well. You would think, for instance, that a mirror that had reflected the face of Washington and heard him swear as he struggled with the intricacies of his satin cravat would never be the same. The beds he slept in never were. They at once became exclusive and proud. But not the mirror. With the indifference of Fate itself it reflected any old face that came along two minutes later. However, we must get on with their history, which is a long and involved one.

Looking-glasses are mentioned in inventories in this country as early as 1650, and probably they were generally used, as they were not difficult to ship from London. In Judge Sewall's famous list of things sent for in 1720 he includes "A True Looking Glass of Black Walnut, Framed in the Newest Fashion (if the Fashion be Good) as good as can be Bought for Five or Six Pounds."

WALNUT MIRRORS—The mirror that Judith's father gave her was probably, at that price, a large one divided in two parts to avoid the tax. The glass was heavy plate with a slight bevel following the outline of the frame. Perhaps there was a star or some such design cut in the upper portion. The frame was black walnut, the upper outline curved, with perhaps a wide cresting above delicately sawed at the edge. Probably the frame was lacquered in

Walnut Mirror

ANTIQUES

gold and bright colours, as that was the "newest fashion" just then. Other mirrors of that type were plain and sometimes without the cresting, but they were always curved at the top, the glass in two sections with the bevelling following the curve of the frame. . . . Do not confuse this early mirror with the one that came in about 1750. It, too, was walnut with the sawed top piece, but the glass was in one piece without bevelling and rectangular in shape, and the decoration was applied in gilt to the top. These are not uncommon. . . . A type still more easily found is mahogany with a bottom as well as a top piece sawed in graceful curlicues. Inside the frame next to the glass is a narrow gilt moulding, and sometimes in the sawed opening at the top is a sort of phenix-looking bird with spread wings, or a shell or flower in gilt. This mirror was in every house from 1770 to 1800. . . .

CONSTITUTION MIRROR—A more elaborate development of the same type shows the "broken arch" with a golden urn or flying eagle at the top. Some of these are very handsome, having besides the eagle delicate carved wood or plaster garlands in gilt along the sides. This is popularly known as the "Constitution Mirror" because it came in about 1776. . . . Straight-top mirrors went through the same evolution as those with the crested tops. In 1725 there was a dignified walnut mirror with the glass in two sections, a straight gilt cornice across the top, and gilt garlands along the sides. . . . In 1780 we have the rectangular all-gilt mirror gracefully festooned with classic garlands in the Adam style. . . . In 1790, we have the Hepplewhite mirror, straight lines, of course, and airy ornaments like wheat or bellflowers in gilt sprouting from an urn at the top. . . .

EMPIRE MIRRORS—By 1800 the familiar Empire mirror began to come in, the glass in two sections again, the upper section marked off with a strip of gilt moulding and painted with the "Frigate Constitution" or some such popular subject. . . . We all know these funny little mirrors with gilt columns at the sides and pressed brass rosettes at the terminals. . . . By 1825 the cornices had projected out into little eaves with golden acorns or balls hanging from them. These mirrors grew and grew into pier glasses as high as the ceiling. . . . Besides the crested saw-top and the straight-top mirrors there were the irregular "fancy" shapes. . . . We will go back and look at Chippendale's. The Chinese designs were rampant at that time, and Chippendale made the most amazing mirrors in that style, covered with scrolls and shells and dripping water and animals and birds and pagodas, all carved and gilded. Many variations of the "Rococo" gilt mirror were made, the French oval with the ribbon bow-knot being one of the most popular.

COURTING MIRROR—Another charming little gilt mirror of about 1790 was called A "Lafayette" or "Courting Mirror." It had a rectangular frame and a cresting at the top, filled in with a picture under glass. There is another curious mirror that has been found in Massachusetts near Marblehead, called the "Balboa" mirror. It is supposed to have been brought home by sailors from the Bay of Biscay. The main portion of the straight rectangular frame is covered with a pinkish sort of stone, like marble. This is glued to the wood and along the edges is a narrow gilt moulding. The fine airy ornaments at the top are made with wire, gilded, and the whole effect is one of peculiar charm. They date from 1770. . . .

GIRANDOLES—The "Girandole," which came in about that time, isn't a mirror at all—that is, it isn't a looking-glass. It is a "circular convex glass in a gilt frame," very elaborate and made in various sizes usually ornamented with the ever-popular eagle. There are branches on each side for candles.

Girandole

Of course, there were many other types and forms of mirrors. Every designer delighted in dallying with the fanciful things, but generally speaking, most of those you find will fall into one or another of these groups.

MOUNTS or BRASSES are a most important item in the study of furniture, and one that is sadly neglected, not only by amateurs, but by many people who consider themselves quite expert in judging old pieces. "These are the original brasses," is a glib phrase that has made more than one good sale for the adroit dealer. "These are the original brasses," repeats the proud purchaser when five times out of ten they not only are not originals, but not even the right ones for the period or the piece.

This is not only sad but stupid. We may be excused for slipping up on other decorative details, but brasses stick right out under our noses and are a most obvious and excellent guide to the honesty of a piece of furniture. Real "original" brasses, such as old hinges and locks, have a look of being wedded to the wood that is very hard to imitate. Years of polishing and wear have literally rubbed them into the surface. Even an old brass mount that has recently been put on will not look the same, in spite of cleverly applied shellac, and new brasses can usually be detected at once.

Of course, the fact that the brasses are wrong does not necessarily mean that the piece is spurious. On the contrary, imitators are careful to have these details right. Very often the owners in former years have changed them themselves. Perhaps they were tired of them and thought that by putting on new mounts the piece would look more in fashion, or one of the originals may have been lost, requiring a whole new set. It is rare, in fact, to find an old piece with all its original brasses, but if they must be replaced, at least we can see that we have the right ones. Early brasses like the iron work were hand-wrought, and the slight irregularities of outline, the quaint but practical shape, and the simple bent staple which often fastened them to the wood, all made for individuality in these ornaments that is quite lacking in the harsh stamped product of to-day.

A description of these little bits of brass would only be confusing. Seeing is believing, so we have made pictures of the most usual and characteristic types for you to look at.

77

N

It is as scandalous for a woman not to know how to use her needle as for a man not to know how to use his sword.
—Lady Mary Wortley Montagu.

NEEDLEWORK is a subject so vast that one despairs of saying anything worth while about it in a few words. It is like trying to count the stars on a summer's night—nice to try but hopeless from the start. Just the same, like the work of the coral-builders, the millions upon millions of stitches picked up on the end of a needle by our patient foremothers went far toward building up the foundation upon which our nation rests, and we cannot possibly pass them by without at least trying to show our respect for them.

Needlework, from the beginning of history, has been the essential occupation of woman, creative and civilizing. With her needle she has been able to satisfy her pride and to show the world what kind of stuff she was made of. No wonder she took it seriously. It is difficult in these machine-driven days for women to understand the passionate, burning interest that women of other days took in their needlework; the peculiar combination of rivalry and pride that kept them bowed over a bit of muslin, taking thirty, fifty, a hundred stitches to the inch! We have better ways, to-day, of proving our worth to the world, but just the same, when we are confronted with one of those amazing quilts or a tiny christening cap, stiff with embroidery, we don't know whether to weep for Hecuba or acknowledge a deep-down secret envy. The needle has slipped from our fingers never to be picked up again. Who can say that we shall ever find an occupation that will satisfy us all, high and low, rich and poor, all over the world, as the needle used to do?

It is impossible, of course, even to touch upon the incredible number of different stitches that can be taken with a needle or the types of design upon which they were used. The best we can do is to pick out a few of the most obvious kinds of needlework and give a brief description of them. Quilts are so important that we have made a separate chapter of them, and perhaps it

ANTIQUES

would be just as well here to confine our attention to what we may call "fancy" work. Obviously the thing to begin with is the sampler.

EARLY EUROPEAN SAMPLERS were just that: a piece of cloth or canvas upon which women worked samples of various designs for future reference. These were the very early kind made by women before there were books of designs. They were very narrow, six or seven inches, and very long, two or three feet, and for convenience' sake were rolled up on ivory or other sticks, and ladies carried them about with them everywhere. When one had a new idea or saw a friend who had, she made a "sample" of it on her sampler. These samplers are without date or name, and some of them, especially those in lace designs, are extraordinarily beautiful. The earliest mention we have of such a sampler is in 1502, and you remember in "A Midsummer Night's Dream" what's-her-name says reproachfully to her supposedly unfaithful friend:

> "We, Hermia, like two artificial gods
> Have with our needles created both one flower,
> Both on one sampler, sitting on one cushion."

It was not until the beginning of the 17th Century that samplers began to have the personal touch—the name, the date, etc.—and to be adorned with dismally pious verses. Perhaps that was the time when mothers first thought of teaching their little girls their letters and text that way. At any rate, women no longer had to make them, for books of designs were out by this time, and the sampler became an exhibition piece of each little girl's ability with her needle.

Poor little kiddies, how they must have slaved over them, driven on by the same insensate pride that made their mothers let them do it! Some of these samplers are marvellous, but I confess that it makes me quite sad to look at them, until I see a little crooked, rebellious, half-finished one that cheers me up.

The oldest sampler we have in this country was made by Loara Standish, who was born in 1623 and died before 1656. She was the daughter of Miles Standish, so he must have recovered from his passion for the beautiful Priscilla and married somebody else. Loara's sampler is done in regular English style in blues and browns, and it hangs to-day in Pilgrim Hall, Plymouth. It reads:

> LORD Guide my Heart that I may do Thy Will
> And fill my heart with such convenient skill
> As will conduce to Virtue void of Shame
> And I will give the glory to Thy Name.
>   Loara Standish is my name.

From that time on samplers were made by every little girl who could hold a needle, and they varied all the way from quite simple ones to the most elaborate and extraordinary. There is no end to the verses, advice, and admonitions worked by those childish fingers. Each one we see seems more quaint and appealing than the last. Many of them are family records, giving the name and date of birth of each member, and as families in those days were often large, the records must have seemed endless to the little workers. Mothers took great pride in the achievements of their little daughters, which in turn reflected their own patience and skill, so samplers were usually well cared for, framed and hung up for all the world to see, and for that reason many of them have come down to us in a state of perfect preservation. They were worked in cross-stitch in bright-coloured wool on homespun linen or on canvas.

There is a great fad for collecting samplers to-day, and their value depends, of course, on the date, the quality and quantity of the work, on their condition, and upon any unique feature in either the work or the design. . . . Samplers should always be kept under glass to preserve them, no matter how simple or crude they are. Don't make use of them for pincushions or table mats, and don't, oh, please don't make covers of them for footstools!

CREWEL-WORK is a very early form of ornamental embroidery and, because it was so simple, effective, and adapted to home-made materials, was very much used by women in our earliest settlements. As Mrs. Wheeler suggests in her delightful book on "Embroidery in America," probably every woman who packed her chest with anxious care before she started on her perilous journey tucked into it somewhere her favourite patterns and bright

ANTIQUES

wools, and brought them out to wile away the long hours on the sunny deck of the *Mayflower*. As soon as ever wool and flax could be raised she began to spin linen and to decorate it with her home-made "crewel" or woollen thread. The matter of colour called upon her utmost ingenuity and skill. The simplest, of course, was to give the wool a dip in the indigo tub that stood in every Colonial back shed—one dip for sky-blue, overnight for dark, which accounts for the great preponderance of blue and white in all early textiles. Brown she got from the walnut tree, yellow from the sumac, green from the bark of young butter-nuts. It was exciting and thrilling work to discover a new source of colour, and when she did find one the goodwife was apt to guard her secret jealously. A good red was the most difficult to get, and there is the story of one woman who found a lovely pink and who went to her grave with her lips shut tight upon her secret. Not very generous, to be sure, but oh, how human!

There were two spinning wheels in every house, the big one for wool, the little one for flax, and how they whirred under the other busy foot that wasn't rocking the baby's cradle! Soon the goodwife's chests were filled with warm homespun for her menfolks and linen for her house, and she had time to think of decoration. Long flowing designs were copied from the India chints that were in most households, or patterns were exchanged and the design sifted through the perforated paper with charcoal on to the white linen beneath. Then she was ready to show what she could do with colours.

The only way to appreciate the marvellous things that were wrought by these remarkable women is to go to some museum and look at them. There are many fine examples to be seen, and they are incredibly lovely. Perhaps the most important work was the hangings and coverings for beds, and we shall speak of them again under "Quilts and Coverlets." Of course, smaller pieces were made, and crewel-work also appears on garments.

As you must have gathered by this time, crewel-work was done on linen in a long and a short flowing stitch, with woollen thread.

TURKEY-WORK was another form of very early decorative work and was in general use from 1645 until the tapestry stitch came along and supplanted it in popularity. It was a coarse heavy work used for cushions and furniture coverings, and nothing more suitable for use with furniture of that early turned variety can be imagined. What has been said above as to wools and dyes holds good here. In this work the heavy worsted yarn was pulled through a coarse cloth, knotted and cut to imitate, as the name applies, the Turkish carpets that were being brought from the Orient. The process resulted in a fabric of unusual charm and durability. Some of it, in perfect condition, exists to-day.

NEEDLEWORK TAPESTRY is the art of reproducing pictures or designs on canvas by stitches in coloured wool. Both Queen Mary, who ascended the English throne in 1689, and Queen Anne, who came shortly after her in 1702, were devoted to that form of needlework, and, of course, all women, high and low, followed their example. The making of tapestry became the passion of the hour. Fine covering for furniture of all sorts, large and small, was the result. This work was called "needlepoint" and was done on canvas in what we call to-day gros point and petit point. Gros point was a true cross-stitch covering two strands of canvas and was used for the heavier parts. Petit point was a half stitch covering only one strand and, when the canvas was very fine, resulting in extraordinarily fine work. This was put into fire screens and similar small pieces, and finer still into the beautiful handbags with which we are familiar to-day. In fact, we are most of us familiar with needlepoint to-day because fortunately there has come another revival of it and much of it is being done. Ten or even five years ago, to find a woman who knew what petit point was would have been like looking—well, for a needle in a haystack. To-day every second woman you meet is busy with it.

It would be nice to go into the history of real tapestry, those magnificent handwoven wall hangings of mediæval times, but this is no place to say more than that needlepoint was inspired by it, and bears about as much relation to it as Turkey-work does to Turkish rugs.

MORAVIAN WORK—There are sure to be women who read this chapter who will want to know where the needlework pictures came from. These

ANTIQUES

quaint examples of stitchery are being very much sought just now, and their history is most interesting. In 1722 a religious group came to America and settled in Pennsylvania. By 1750 their schools had become the birthplace of fine needlework in America. They taught, not only tambour, fine white embroidery, ribbon work, crêpe work, flower embroidery, etc., but the making of pictures with a needle on satin. These were made on a frame with the long (what is known as the Kensington) stitch. In the late 18th and early 19th centuries this work became extremely popular. It just suited the romantic and sentimental ladies of that time who found tapestry much, much too heavy for their lily-white hands. Many types of pictures of this kind were made, some of them Bible subjects, some family groups with the faces painted separately on cardboard and worked in with the hair of the beloved subjects, but the most numerous of them were what might be called mourning pieces: pictures of graves and monuments overhung with weeping willows and weeping females. The inscriptions on the graves were usually inked in and were probably authentic! Still others were copies of prints of famous places. A friend of mine has an exquisite one of Mount Vernon; at least she believed it to be Mount Vernon, but there was no portico. Recently, being a lover of old prints, she visited an exhibition of rare and costly ones. There, in a place of honour, was a mezzotint, the exact duplicate of her needlework picture, tree for tree, grass blade for grass blade—but with a full-fledged portico. In great excitement she rushed home and again, more carefully than ever, examined her picture, and there, faintly traced in pencil, was the portico. It had never been finished. The picture had been done by an early aunt whose father was a friend of Lafayette and one of the first men to help preserve Mount Vernon as a national monument. Rather nice to have, wouldn't you say?

Needlework pictures were made between 1775 and 1830–40. Usually the date can be fairly accurately placed by the subject, like the Mount Vernon one, for instance, or by the costumes of the figures. On many of the mourning ones we find dates on the tombstones. While these things do not, of course, give the exact hour of the completion of the work, they are a fairly good guide to its age.

EMBROIDERY ON WHITE—At no time in the history of the world—that is, in modern history—was there more elaboration in the matter of dress than between 1700 and 1850. Fabrics were gorgeous and the styles calculated to display them to the utmost advantage. Think of the Court of Louis XVI, for example. It is difficult to-day to get any conception of the beauty and elaborateness of these garments. Not only were they of fine materials, exquisitely fashioned, but they were heavily encrusted with embroidery in silk and in gold and silver. We cannot go into it in detail here, more than to point out that over here in America we were "keeping up with Marie" to the best of our ability. We, too, had our silks and brocades and embroideries, our satin waistcoats, velvet coats, and satin dresses, although to no such extent as they had abroad. Perhaps the most beautiful work that has come down to us, however, was upon white. Long christening dresses of babies, their tiny caps and coats of fine India mull, are stiff with embroidery of the most remarkable fineness and delicacy. Embroidered kerchiefs were much worn and women's muslin dresses were one mass of needlework. Hemstitched ruffles of fine linen were worn by men as well as women, and it was a matter of pride that these should always be immaculate. Narrow rolls of muslin and linen and skeins of fine thread went everywhere with women. The designs were stamped, "stuffed," and then worked with the cross-over satin stitch, just as we do to-day—when we occasionally attempt a bit of work between rounds of golf or bridge or after hours at the office. I fear, however, that future generations will never point with pride to our endeavours. We haven't the time. I remember once saying that to an old gentleman of what we call the "old school." He smiled benignly and remarked, "You have as much time as Shakespeare had." Well, perhaps we have, and as much as those women had, too, but it seems to go somewhere. One early writer in a panic expressed the fear that the "acquirement of book learning by women will make them neglect their needlework." He seems to have been a far-sighted sort of person!

O

They also serve who only stand and wait.
—MILTON: "Sonnets."

OCCASIONAL PIECES are the little things in between that fill up the chinks and cement the home together. It isn't the big important pieces that make for charm; it is the dainty trifles that go with them. That is why the usual museum exhibit is so cold. The pieces are fine, much finer than we can hope to have in our homes, but they look stiff and unhappy because they lack the intimate touch of little things. This is sometimes true of the homes of people who make collections. Their love for the unusual and rare is apt to make them forget that antiques lose their charm, at least to the home-lover, unless they are put to use. I would rather have one teapot on the table before the fire than a hundred on a shelf around the picture moulding.

Occasional pieces are intimate because they are small. People may change their big pieces for bigger ones, but they cling to the little ones. We have spoken in other places of small tables, lamps, needlework, and such like things, that really are occasional pieces, but there are a few more that do not fit in anywhere, and we will put them together here.

Cricket Stool

FOOTSTOOLS are a very early form of furniture, and Necessity, as so often happens, was their mother. Along in Queen Elizabeth's time people got tired of hooking their heels to the stretchers of chairs to keep them off the cold and dirty floor, so someone made a footstool. From that day to this, until steam heat made their use an affectation, footstools have been constantly in use. . . . The early Jacobean chairs were made high on purpose so that footstools could be used with them, and the stools, like the chairs, were made of oak or walnut with turned or scrolled legs and sometimes a cane seat to match the chair.

Sometimes, instead of legs, the stool rested on bench ends. Our early American ones were often made like that, or with four stout little legs set at an angle into the solid seat. These were called "crickets" perhaps because they sat on the hearth. . . . Early in the 18th Century footstools became more elaborate and were covered with brocade or velvet or with the needlepoint that women made. There was not much to change about these little pieces, but they did their best to follow the fashions, turning up with ball-and-claw feet in Chippendale's time, with delicate curves and inlay in Sheraton's, and becoming square and solid with a thick superstructure of upholstery in haircloth or needlework in the Empire. . . . Although we have little use for them to-day in our busy lives and in our steam-heated rooms, footstools are coming back just because we like them. You can find the soft wools and old designs for needlework covers for them in almost any shop where ten years ago you would have looked for them in vain.

FIRE SCREENS are very like footstools in intimate character and they have always been close companions by the fireside. While footstools were made to protect the feet from the cold, screens were to protect the face from the heat. They are not as old as footstools, coming in about Chippendale's time, and they are rarely seen now. (The modern adaptation of the fire screen is a wire mesh to prevent sparks from flying out into the room.) Chippendale gave a great deal of care to fire screens and did much to increase their popularity. They were made in two types, called the pole screen and the horse screen

Needlework Footstool

Haircloth Footstool

Horse Screen

POLE SCREEN was a slender mahogany standard on a tripod base, the delicate "snake" feet weighted with lead to keep it from upsetting. Attached to the pole was a square, or in Sheraton's time a heart-shaped frame, that could be lifted up and down. It was in this frame that ladies placed their finest bits of needlework or embroidery on satin, for there it would show to the utmost advantage. These dainty little screens were meant to protect only the face from the devastating heat of the flames, but when something more was needed to protect the body as well, the horse screen was used.

HORSE SCREEN—This was no more than two uprights supporting a good-sized rectangular panel filled in with the same fine needlework. The panel slid up and down in grooves, and when Sheraton came along, with his usual ingenuity, he made one that would turn in the frame so that it could be adjusted without moving the whole thing. . . . The variation and interest in both types of screen come, of course, from the difference in workmanship and in the needlework. Most of them were exceedingly graceful and delicate. Those used in this country were for the most part imported. They are distinctly an English bit.

CANDLE STANDS really belong with tables, but they have so much in common with footstools and fire screens that they will perhaps be more comfortable here. They came in very early, as would be natural when candles were in use, and at first were crude and simple, just an upright with a small top and a criss-cross base to keep them steady. They were made of iron, too, and we mentioned those under "Lamps and Lighting." But in Chippendale's time they became very graceful, much like the pole screens in character, a delicate carved standard on a tripod base and with a small round top on which to put the candlestick. With Hepplewhite and Sheraton they became even more lovely, and Hepplewhite says of them "they are very useful—a light can be placed in any part at pleasure, in drawing rooms, halls, and on large staircases." . . . Fortunately these lovely stands are as useful to-day as they ever were —for candlelight or for a bowl of flowers or a bit of ivy in a quiet corner. The old ones are rare and high in price, but lovely ones can be made from a single post from an old "four-poster"— a most satisfactory way to do a bit of rescue work.

Chippendale Candlestand

P

*O, good old man, how well in thee appears
The constant service of the antique world!*
—SHAKESPEARE: "As You Like It."

DUNCAN PHYFE is the most interesting character in the whole history of American furniture making. He was not only the greatest but the only great cabinet maker that America has ever produced, but strangely enough, until recently, his very name, much less his furniture, was little known except to a few astute collectors. Now, however, the pendulum has swung the other way—as pendulums have a habit of doing—and there is a great vogue for "Phyfe" furniture. Unfortunately, although he worked for many years, few pieces of genuine Phyfe have come to light, and as these are all privately owned or in museums, the only way we can have this beautiful and representative furniture in our homes is to reproduce it. So far very few reproductions have been made and those that do appear are often sold as genuine. However, the canny cabinet maker has his ear pretty close to the ground, and it will not be long before both fakes and honest reproductions will come out in abundance.

Duncan Phyfe, like his great predecessor Robert Adam, was a Scotsman. He came to America in 1784 when he was a lad of sixteen and lived with his father in Albany, where he learned the trade of cabinet making. This was the only training he ever had, and in comparing his work with that of the "Big Four"—and the best of it does compare favourably with theirs—it is only fair to remember all the advantages of tradition and association that they had. Phyfe came to New York as a young man and set up a little shop in Broad Street, where he began turning out his beautiful cabinet work. He was a little man, proud and stubborn, painstaking and slow. Perhaps his very exclusiveness made him popular, for after severe early struggles he succeeded in attracting a wealthy clientèle. He never became independent, however, although at one time he employed as many as one hundred men in his shop.

Phyfe's work may be divided into three periods: from 1795 to 1818, from 1818 to 1830, and from 1830 to 1847. He produced his finest work during the first period. Just across the water in England, Sheraton was working, too, and to a certain extent Phyfe came under his influence, but although he has been called the "American Sheraton," Phyfe had too much personality of his own to be very vitally influenced by any one. There is a total absence of light wood, inlay, and painting in Phyfe's work, and certainly Sheraton never used the long sweeping concave curve that Phyfe employed so frequently on table and chair legs. There is something of Adam in the classic "lyre" design he used so much in chair backs and pedestals, and in the nice placing of decoration, something, too, of Chippendale in the fact that he used mahogany almost exclusively and that carving was his chief decoration, but after all, there is a quality in Phyfe's work that is not quite the classic coldness of Adam, or the aristocracy of Sheraton, or the hearty largeness of Chippendale; a kind of painstaking dryness, an honesty and restraint that are characteristic of the man himself. You may never be wildly enthusiastic about Phyfe's furniture, but you are bound to respect it.

During the depression that followed the War of 1812 even the wealthy were reluctant to pay the price for Phyfe's scrupulous work and high-grade materials, especially as he stuck stubbornly to the old styles when the rest of the world was going wild over the Empire idea. He held back splendidly from the popular demand, and it is due to his restraining influence that American Empire never did descend to quite the depths to which furniture plunged in Europe. Gradually, however, he allowed a touch of Empire to creep in, and after 1830, in order to make a living, he at last produced the kind of heavy stuff that people wanted. From that time on, until he retired in 1847, his work deteriorated into what he himself bitterly called "butcher furniture."

The love of Phyfe's life was mahogany. He understood the wood and laboured all his years to bring out its beauty. He was so particular about the quality of his logs that down in the West Indies the finest timbers became known as "Duncan Phyfe's." He seasoned his wood in his backyard, cutting it himself with the utmost care. One can imagine him, a "tight" little man in a canvas apron, his pipe in his mouth, bending over it, scrutinizing the grain or carefully fitting a bit of fine veneer, indifferent to the wealthy customer who came picking his way through the litter of the shop, tossing the long curling shavings from the tip of a gold-headed cane. The fact that Phyfe never catered to fashion kept him poor all his life; but it also made him a great man.

When he was eighty years old he retired, but it is said that even then he had a bench at home where he worked away carving and polishing bits of fine mahogany until he died in 1854 at the age of eighty-six. A grande gude mon was Duncan Phyfe, American!

PEWTER has a history almost as long and honourable as that of glass, but if we go back to the Romans that ought to be far enough. They made it and so did all the other peoples who were struggling into national formation during the Dark and Middle Ages. Apparently it was easy to make and shape, being made of tin with lead added to cheapen and make it malleable, and except for wooden trenchers and leather mugs, pewter utensils were those most commonly used for centuries.

It is first mentioned in history as being permitted for use in the Cathedral at Rouen in 1074. Two hundred years later pewter caldrons were used for boiling meat at the coronation of Edward the First. In 1348 a Pewterers Guild was formed in London to regulate the quality of pewter, the best to consist of tin with the addition of as much brass as the "tin of its own nature" would take. Articles made from this were called "vessels of tin forever." The poorer quality contained from 20 to 40 per cent. lead—deadly containers for food. In 1475—but who cares what the pewterers did in 1475? Let us get on to pewter in America!

By the time the Colonists sailed for America pewter had largely supplanted the wooden trencher and was in common use for household purposes all over Europe. We find it mentioned among the first things "to send for Newe England" on the shipping lists of 1629, and quantities of it continued to come in for the next two hundred years. All the early wills and inventories mention pewter in considerable quantities and in all manner of forms. One prosperous merchant of Salem who died in 1647 had in his kitchen "twenty-two platters, two great plates and ten little ones, one great pewter pot, one flagon, one bottle, one quart, three pints, four ale quarts, six beer cups, four wine cups, four candle sticks, five chamber pots, two lamps, one funnel, six saucers and miscellaneous old pewter, the whole valued at £7." Other lists contain spoons, salts, basins, fruit dishes, porringers, trays, in fact, all household utensils not subjected to intense heat or to pressure—like forks, which would bend.

But in spite of the fact that pewter was so much used, there seems to have been few professional pewterers here much before the middle of the 18th Century. We do find mention of one itinerant tinker who went about mending the handles of spoons, which broke easily, and patching up pieces that had melted. His name was Richard Graves, and he must have been quite a rascal, for he was arrested once in 1642 for "oppression in his trade of pewtering," again for calling his neighbour "a base fellow and ye might Runn a half pike in his bellie and never touch his hart," and again because one William Allen testified that "he herd Rich Graves kissed Goody Gent twice." When Richard confessed that this was true he was whipped and made to sit in the stocks. Take it all in all, I think poor Richard deserves a place somewhere in the history of pewtering!

Probably the first pewter made in America was cast in moulds rather crudely by individuals, but by the middle of the 18th Century there were many professional pewterers. Although some of the early work is very fine, the names of the makers are lost and we know of no outstanding master of the craft, as we do in furniture making or in silver or in glass. The early pewter was the best because it was the simplest. The makers did not attempt to go outside the limits of their material, the forms were simple with the hammer marks showing in naïve decoration on the soft gray lustrous material, but although it was commonly used, especially in the rural districts, there is very little early pewter to be found. Much of it was melted and turned into bullets during the Revolution, and much more was chucked out on the junk heap after it went out of fashion.

After 1780 the alloy deteriorated and so did the forms. The makers made the mistake of trying to imitate silver, with the result that pewter became neither fish, nor flesh, nor good red herring. Gradually, between silver on one hand and china on the other, pewter gave up the ghost. By 1825 its use was practically superseded by chinaware, and by 1850, after a long service beginning with all the pomp and pageantry of princes and priests and ending in the humbleness of simple homes, it entirely disappeared. Now, after an oblivion of nearly a hundred years, it is coming back again. Fine pewter, especially early pewter, is undoubtedly very lovely, but it is exceedingly difficult to find. The early hall mark or "touch," very often in the form of a spread eagle, sometimes with the maker's name but more often not, is being faked, and as it is easy and profitable to make perfect imitations of early pewter, a great deal of it is on the market, and it is exceedingly difficult to detect the old from the new. Look out for fake porringers, flagons, plates, and whale-oil lamps. On the other hand, faked or not, I know of nothing more wistfully appealing than pewter in an old-fashioned home; a plate filled with oranges on your maple table, a whale-oil lamp with a little pleated shade, will lend a touch of gentleness and charm found nowhere but in this soft gray ghost among metals. Pewter is longing to come back. Let us lend it a helping hand for old time's sake.

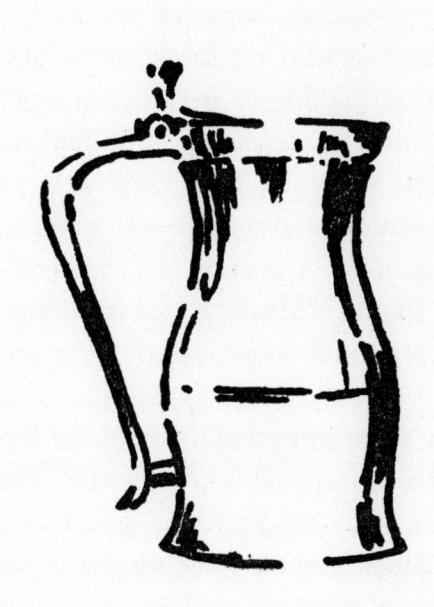

Q

Home to my poor wife who works all day like a horse at the makings of her hangings for our chamber and bed.
—SAMUEL PEPYS: "Diary"

QUILTS and COVERLETS—Ever since we left beds, away back in the B's, I have been wanting to get to quilts and coverlets and the hangings that made the bed so important in the old days. Perhaps it is insinctive to want to get those beds "made up," for no good housewife is easy in her mind until that task is done. And what a task it must have been, beating up to fluffiness and spreading smooth the great feather beds, stretching taut the wide homespun linen sheets, shaking out the coverlets, arranging the flowered spread of chintz or crewel-work and tying back the draperies. But when it was all done, how magnificent to survey, and how comfortable to climb into! In these days of steam heat and box springs the idea of diving into billows of feathers is anything but appealing, but if you will remember what living conditions were like in those days, how cold and draughty the rooms were, that there were no such things as springs, that the only spot in the house where one could stretch out and rest was in bed, you will find that the Colonial housewife did pretty well. As a matter of fact, the bed was the most important feature in her house, and on it she lavished all her energy and pride. She literally, as the invaluable Pepys says, worked like a horse over it, and the results of her labours fill us with wonder and admiration to-day.

Bed furnishings are given first place in all the early inventories, especially feather beds, which were sometimes valued as high as all the rest of the house furnishings put together. There is much mention of curtains, testers, and "valients," the colour often red or "grene" or "sad," but there is not much mention of material to guide us. The word "calico" appears very often and this undoubtedly meant the printed India chintz that had recently become very popular in England. Pepys—again—has an entry, September 5, 1663: "Bought my wife a chint, that is, a painted East India calico for to line her new study." Calico, by the way, was the name given to these materials by the Portuguese traders who were the first to bring them to Europe, and "chint" is an Indian word meaning coloured or variegated. Many of these charming India draperies were brought to the Colonies and used on beds and at the windows. Imitation India draperies were afterward printed in England and in France, the famous Toile de Jouy being the most beautiful. This cloth (toile) was first printed by a man named Oberkampf in the little village of Jouy near Versailles in the year 1738.

Besides the calico or chintz the Colonial housewife had hangings of serge, "blew harrateen," "linceys," etc., such as were used on English four-posters at that time, and if she were the wife of the Governor or of a prosperous merchant, handsome damask or silk ones. "Silke blankets" and "counterpanes" are often mentioned, and a "stript blanket" may have been a woven coverlet.

CREWEL HANGINGS—But the hanging most beautiful and typical of the times was the lovely crewel-work, done, as we have described under "Needlework," on homespun linen with coloured wool. Not only was this entirely home made, which makes it doubly precious, but the designs copied from the Indian chintz were exquisitely flowing and graceful. Some few, a very few of these lovely works of art are cherished in our museums and are well worth a moment's pause, a silent tribute as we hurry by.

TUFTED and KNOTTED HANGINGS—It is extremely difficult to be definite about needlework, and foolish to try to be. Who can tell when the first woman thought of drawing a bit of candle wicking through her cotton or linen homespun and snipping it off in a tuft, like Turkey-work? Who was she who went her one better by making a "drawed in" spread with the loops pulled through like a hooked rug? Was it the wife of a fisherman who started the craze for knotted fringe? And where was the grim-faced woman who first sat down, determined to knit a whole bedspread? It is impossible to know these things. The secret of them lies buried beneath the toppling, moss-covered stones in many a New England churchyard with the dust that was once so full

ANTIQUES

of pride and energy. And why should we be so pedantic about it? Better remember and revere the spirit that was behind the work than fuss about dates. All we can say about those simple, home-made spreads and hangings, the tufted and fringed and knotted ones so charming on "field" beds, is that they were "early," probably taking the place of crewel-work and chintz when the Revolution made old ideas detestable. Such simple light draperies were used on four-posters until those beds went out of style about 1830.

COVERLETS—While woven coverlets were undoubtedly made by the first woman to turn a spinning wheel in this country, the great majority of those we see to-day, the blue and white, or brown and red, or red, white, and blue, were made about 1800. After the Revolution there was a great migration out of New England into the wilderness of Tennessee, Kentucky, and Virginia, and it is in the mountains there that most of the finest coverlets and quilts are found. Of course, they were made before that in New England and continued to be made there, but it was in the lonely cabins, far from towns, that the loveliest ones came into the world. They are found there, literally, by the hundreds, the colours still bright, the patterns marvels of ingenuity. And such wistful names as those women gave them, "Sunrise on the Walls of Troy," "Governor's Garden," Blazing Star," "Lonely Heart"; or as they worked unnoticed listening to the talk around the fire, perhaps they wove "Washington's Ring," "Lafayette's Fancy," "Tennessee Trouble," or "Lee's Surrender" into their "kivers." If they were still young they may have had a little quiet fun out of "Catch Me if You Can," "Hen Scratch," or "Drunkard's Path." There are hosts of patterns with these delightful names.

They carded, spun, and dyed the wool just as the earliest Puritan women did, looking for dyes in the roots and bark of trees. After about 1830 much of the weaving was done by itinerant weavers who came each year to a district, set up their looms, and wove blankets from the balls of wool that had been prepared for them. Some of these men were famous for their remarkable work, and many of their elaborate double blankets are signed and dated in one corner, but while these coverlets are extremely handsome with spread eagles and

"E Pluribus Unum" about the borders, they lack the simple charm of the home-made ones.

For many years woven coverlets were sadly neglected, perhaps because they were just "home made" and didn't count. They were used as horse blankets, floor coverings, anywhere a good strong rug was needed, but such was their splendid quality that they have hung together even to this day, the "Sunrise on the Walls of Troy" still softly glimmering. Every one of them deserves the greatest care, and they should be rescued at every opportunity.

QUILTS—Patchwork and quilting go back, of course, to the time of Pharaoh, and marvellous quilted garments, appliquéd in gold and silver, were worn in the 15th and 16th centuries, as you may see, for example, in Velasquez's painting of the little Infanta. But how much quilting was done in the very early Colonies we will never know, for none of it remains to tell the tale. Quilted petticoats are mentioned in a Boston newspaper in 1707, but there our information stops. Undoubtedly, however, a great deal of it was done because the Colonial women from England and Holland were accustomed to it at home and were sure to fly to it as soon as the heavy work was done.

Patchwork and piecework from which quilts are made have always appealed very much to women who have little leisure for "fancy" work. Their consciences are free because they are doing something "useful," and at the same time they can indulge themselves to their hearts' content in fanciful designs and colours. Even more than in crewel-work or in woven coverlets or in hooked rugs, a woman could let her fancy loose on a patchwork quilt. There were so many bits of cloth, such bright colours to choose from, so many ways of putting them together. She could arrange and rearrange. There was no limit to what she might do, and some of the quilts are marvellous as a result. Moreover, patchwork and piecework could be carried about. She did not have to sit at the old loom to do it. She could go and visit or, if she were alone, sit on the step and watch the sunset over the Blue Ridge while her fingers hurried mechanically around the edges of a patch.

Perhaps it would be as well to explain the difference between patchwork

ANTIQUES

and piecework quilts. Someone has said that "piecework quilts were a woman's daily task; patchwork quilts her glory," but I do not know about that. I have made both myself—not very grand ones, to be sure—but enough to know that it is about as much fun to put together the exact geometrical designs as it is to "lay down" the freer designs in patchwork.

A piecework quilt is made of many pieces of material cut into squares and sewed together into diamonds or stars or blocks or any other design made up of straight lines.

A patchwork quilt is one upon which the design is laid on like a "patch" and sewed into place. In other words, the design, leaves, flowers, or what you will, is cut separately and applied (appliquéd) to the quilt. Of course, this permits of much more freedom of fancy, and slight irregularities only add to the beauty of the work.

After the patchwork or piecework has been finished it is ready to be quilted. It is then stretched out taut upon a frame and a thin layer of cotton laid between it and the plain cloth underneath. The lines for the stitches that hold them together are then drawn, the straight lines "snapped" on with a string dipped in chalk, the circles outlined in pencil around the edge of a cup perhaps, or if a more elaborate design is desired—an arrow or leaf—it is cut from cardboard and the tracing made around that.

Then the quilting begins, those endless, endless stitches! Sometimes in the old days it was given to a woman who made quilting her life's work. She was paid, not for the amount of quilting she got through, but for the amount of thread she used, which may account for some of the amazing work on some of the old quilts. The way to beat that game was to take forty or fifty stitches to the inch! Or if the quilters lived in a village it was often the custom for each to finish her piecework at about the same time, and then all of them, ten or twelve, got together in "quilting bees," sitting around the frame gossiping, with a sharp eye on each other's stitches. But more often the woman who did the patching did the quilting, too, working alone with a queer fierce pride in her stitches, filling up her life from the cradle to the grave with these extraordinary creations of her stifled imagination and work-worn fingers.

PADDED and CORDED QUILTS—About 1800 there was a rage for white bed coverings—which has lasted, come to think of it, until the present day—which gave great impetus to knitted and crocheted ones. Most of us have such bedspreads in our families dating from about 1810 or so. But the most extraordinary production of that time, and perhaps the most amazing of all quilts, was the white padded and corded one. As there was no colour to enliven these quilts the women proceeded to decorate them by raising the pattern from the surface by stuffing it. This was done apparently in two ways: either the cord was sewed in a pattern on to the coarse, loose-woven foundation cloth, the fine cambric then laid over it and sewed down on both sides of the cord, thus raising the pattern to the surface, or the two cloths were laid together, the pattern sewed into them and the cord drawn through afterward. Imagine the incredible exactness of such work! The petals and leaves of flowers were first outlined in a running stitch, after which the coarse underlining was parted with some blunt instrument like a knitting needle and cotton poked into the pattern until it was "fat" enough to please the worker. Really! They made big spreads that way, covered with design, one mass of stitches. And bureau covers and "splashers" to match! One looks at this work and gasps. It doesn't seem possible. And yet, somehow, in spite of all the patience shown, the loveliness of pattern, and the incredible fineness of the work, it does not begin to have the appeal of crewel- or patch- or piecework. One cannot say why, but it seems somehow to have lost in imagination and become sophisticated, a conscious effort to show how very good and wonderful the worker was. Well, so she was. So is the man who balances five oranges on his nose, but, after all, one finds oneself wondering what he is doing it for, anyhow!

That ends Quilts and Coverlets. After the padded and corded quilt nothing further *could* happen. But even to this day, in out-of-the-way places you find women still making piecework quilts, the last feeble glimmer of a glorious past.

R

*Such pretie things would soon be gon,
If we should not so them remembre.*

—ANONYMOUS.

RESTORATION and CARE—Many people are deeply interested in rescuing antiques, pulling them out of barns and attics, scraping off the stains from weather or ill use, exclaiming rapturously over the wonders hidden beneath innumerable coats of paint, eagerly restoring old pieces to their early usefulness and beauty. This is a splendid thing and our enthusiasm for it must never lag for a moment. No matter how hopeless a piece may look, how decrepit and broken, if there is the least trace of beauty in it, try to save it every time.

In the first place, that is the only way really to know and love your pieces. If you have them drop like plums into your lap, all shining and bright, you cannot even guess at their early history, which is often the most interesting part about them, and you can never be quite, quite sure that they are just exactly what they look. Therefore, although it is becoming more and more difficult, try to find and restore your own antiques, so far as you are able. And cheer up, for wonderful things may happen. Only last week I saw a five-slat Pennsylvania chair in almost perfect condition that had been bought at an auction for five dollars. Out in the same lucky man's barn was a fine Dutch *kas*, black with paint, but with some of the original decoration still gleaming through. Fine things can still be found, only you may have to look a little harder and pay a little more for them.

But—and it is a large but, too—just how far can restoration go and still leave you with an honest old piece? That is a question that has been argued threadbare and will never be answered, except by every man to himself.

Of course, when all of the parts are there, all the legs and panels and drawers, needing only to be reassembled and put in order, such a piece, when it is finished, is unquestionably an "original." It would be rare, indeed, to find any piece of great age that did not need some work done upon it. If the upholstery is gone, or part of the inlay missing, even a very large part—all of it!—you may still feel that your piece is original. If the brasses are gone or part of the moulding, a stretcher or a spindle or two—umm, yes! *But* if the legs, one or two, are gone, or a drawer, or an important panel, what then? This is where opinions differ. Of course, such a piece would not be admitted into a museum as an original, and many experts would call it "restored"—which it is—only the word carries such a stigma with it. It seems to me that if the body of the piece is there, so that the feeling and character are not destroyed, you can go a long way with restoration and still feel that you have an old piece. But when a whole high-boy is built around one drawer or a back and legs added to an old seat, no one resents more bitterly than I having such a piece palmed off as original.

So far as many dealers are concerned, the slightest crumb of original wood is sufficient to appease their consciences, so that the word "original" often means very, very little.

The restoration of a fine old piece is a serious matter and much harm can be done by enthusiastic bungling. As Hawthorne indignantly said when they wanted to paint his old Manse, "The hand that renovates is more sacrilegious than that which destroys." And there is a great deal in it. Many beautiful pieces have been ruined by ignorant handling. Try to find someone you can trust with the work and then watch him like a hawk! If the piece has never been painted or subjected to the hideous liquid polish that, around 1800, was put on many old pieces and which left a sort of greenish black tinge on the surface, do not under any circumstances let him scrape your piece. Altogether too much scraping is being done. Every old piece of maple or cherry or even mahogany is scraped down to the bone, which gives it a bright new finish and utterly destroys the soft *patine* that only time can give—a terrible pity! Of course, if the piece has been burned or painted or has that dreadful polish on it, the only thing to do is scrape it off, and begin patiently to bring back the *patine*. It will come—with time.

ANTIQUES

CARE—The very people who really love old furniture and who seek diligently until they find it are sometimes strangely apathetic once they have captured and got it in their homes. They simply place it in the proper spot and beam at it. Seasons come and seasons go, and except for a superficial dusting with a light cloth the piece is never touched. After a time, and not a very long time, either, they notice with horror that the piece is cracking, the veneer is popping out, the drawers won't close, the wood loses its lustre and becomes dull and unhappy looking. The whole piece seems to have lost life.

That is exactly what has happened. The piece is starved from lack of care.

In European countries, where old furniture is the rule rather than the exception, it is a well-understood thing that wood has to be "fed." In fact, there is an old English proverb which says, "You must feed the oak with oil and polish it with wax"—an excellent rule to remember.

Perhaps it would be interesting to know something about how old furniture was finished, which may make the process of caring for it clearer.

Much early furniture, Elizabethan and Jacobean, was given no surface finish whatsoever except the rubbing that would come naturally from weeks and months of hand labour on the carving and finishing of it. The custom of treating it with oil and coating it with beeswax gradually became universal, all woods being treated in the same way. They were first given an application of oil which was allowed to dry on for some hours, or better still, for a day. The surface was then wiped off thoroughly, removing all the oil not absorbed by the wood. Beeswax was then rubbed in and polished with a woollen rag. A thin coating of shellac was sometimes given to walnut furniture before the wax was applied, which accounts for the fact that much early walnut is riddled with wormholes, the worms being attracted by the shellac. Walnut that has never been treated with anything but wax is much freer from the ravages of these miserable pests. Mahogany, when it came along, was treated to the same doses of oil and wax, and it is the beautiful finish left by years of this treatment that we call the "original *patine*." This *patine*, or surface finish, is a reliable guide to the age of a piece of furniture, since time alone can bring about the true mellowness and colour of it. Once recognized it can never be mistaken.

About 1800 following in the wake of Hepplewhite's "very elegant fashion" of "japanning" his furniture with thin, clear shellac, a high, hard, almost metallic finish became very popular, and many old pieces were given a coat of liquid polish over the fine old *patine*—a most unhappy error. These are the pieces that must be scraped and the *patine* started all over again. If you have such a piece or one that has been painted proceed with it in this manner:

After all the varnish or paint has been removed, treat it at frequent intervals to doses of *boiled* linseed oil, as much of the oil being immediately rubbed off as does not soak into the wood. Repeat this every few days, every week, every two weeks, until the wood gradually assumes the look of being well fed. When this is accomplished begin rubbing it with wax, as will be described in a moment, and slowly but surely the piece will assume a *patine* very like the old. This is a long task, but the result is well worth the trouble and time, not only because of the added beauty but because such a surface is never injured by liquids being spilled upon it. A little rubbing with the boiled oil will always remove all stains. Sometimes a white spot will be caused by a hot plate. This can be removed by brushing lightly and *quickly* with pure alcohol. The best way to do this is to have a piece of dry cheesecloth in one hand and a piece moistened with alcohol in the other, as lightning speed is necessary, or the spot will be burned.

If you are lucky enough to have a piece with the original *patine* intact, a different method is used. All these pieces need is to be rubbed and polished with wax.

There is a most excellent wax already prepared, called "Partridge's Wax," but if you cannot obtain this, mix a little turpentine with beeswax, just enough to soften the wax. Then proceed in this manner.

Apply the wax with a cloth and rub it in thoroughly with a good stiff brush; not a coarse brush, but one that will stand up under considerable pressure. Scrub up and down, *with the grain of the wood*, until the wax has thoroughly penetrated the pores. Then wrap your brush up in a soft cloth and rub

ANTIQUES

off the wax that remains on the surface, and you will have a most beautiful, lustrous, soft polish. This applies to flat surfaces, inlaid or plain. Carving, of course, must be got at as best you can, and the little wax that remains in the creases only adds the charm of a deeper colour to the decoration. Book bindings and leather chair coverings are greatly improved by the same treatment, as the wax keeps them soft and prevents cracking.

Extreme changes of temperature are very harmful to old furniture, and so is dry heat. Fresh air and an even cool temperature are absolutely essential to the life of such pieces. After all, they are vegetable substance and will wither and go to dust without air. Beware, on the other hand, of too much moisture, for a piece that has once warped can seldom be brought into shape again. One way to avoid warping, especially if you are leaving your furniture shut up for some time, in the summer or in storage, is to place bricks wrapped in cloth on all the suspicious corners. Keep doors locked and drawers completely closed. It is a good idea to paste a small label inside the drawers—"Please push this drawer in as far as you can"—a gentle hint to those who otherwise might be careless. The care of old furniture is not only a pleasure but a very real duty, especially in America, where the atmospheric conditions are against it from the start. *Noblesse oblige*. It is churlish and dishonourable, after a piece has been cared for and cherished for many years, to allow it to go to pieces after it has come into our hands.

S

His time is forever, everywhere his place.
—Cowley: "Friendship in Absence."

SHERATON brings us to the last of the "Big Four" and, in the opinion of many, to the greatest of them. Certainly no name, except that of Chippendale, is more familiar to lovers of furniture, and no one, not even Chippendale, had more influence on furniture styles here in America, past and present. The reasons for this are quite obvious. Sheraton's designs combined lightness and grace with strength; they have distinction without being obtrusive, size without bigness, and they call for no particular "period" treatment in decoration. Also, they are invariably in good taste. They are "safe." Naturally, they appeal, not only to the fastidious, but to the practical mind as well. It goes without saying that we ought to be able to recognize the "Sheraton influence" the moment we see it, and that we should know something of the man who created it.

Thomas Sheraton was born of humble parentage at Stockton-on-Tees in 1750, came to London in 1790, and died there in 1806. By the time he got to London, Chippendale had been dead for eleven years, and Hepplewhite for four. Adam died two years later. Hepplewhite's shop, however, under the name of A. Hepplewhite & Co., was still flourishing, and his book of designs, published by his widow, had appeared in 1788.

In 1791 Sheraton brought out his book of designs, which was eagerly taken up by the cabinet makers of the day. In it Sheraton clinched the tendency for classic design which had come in with Adam and had been carried forward by Hepplewhite. Sheraton, like Adam, was a lover of straight clean lines and classic decoration. He used painting to some extent, as Adam did, but not nearly so much as Hepplewhite, preferring instead the beautiful veneer and delicate inlay for which he is famous. He used satin-wood extensively.

But we have described his furniture types under other headings and must confine ourselves here to what little is known of the man himself.

Sheraton was born poor and died poor. His life was one long struggle, bravely sustained, during which he never for a moment relinquished his ideals. At an early age he showed a marked ability for drawing which he steadily cultivated, and this, combined with his practical training at the bench, laid the foundation for his future work. Added to this he had an unerring sense of proportion and instinctive good taste, but although he describes himself in his books as a cabinet maker, it is believed that he did very little actual cabinet work after he got to London. Certainly he had no such shop as Chippendale's or Hepplewhite's, but lived in miserable poverty in Soho, where he executed his beautiful designs for other people to work from, wrote his books, taught, and preached. In the Memoirs of Adam Black we find a saddening glimpse of Sheraton in his last years: "He [Sheraton] lived in a poor street—his house half shop, half dwelling—and looked a Methodist preacher worn out, with threadbare black coat." Black must have worked with Sheraton in some capacity, for he says later: "I wrought among dirt and bugs. . . . Miserable as the payment was, I was ashamed to take it from the poor man. . . . He is a man of talent and, I believe, genuine piety. He understands the cabinet business—I believe was bred to it. He is a scholar, writes well, and in my opinion, draws masterly; is an author, bookseller, and preacher. We may be ready to ask how comes it to pass that a man of such abilities and resources is in such a state?"

Alas, how comes it, indeed? What was lacking in that upright and sensitive soul, that fertile imagination and inquiring mind that kept Sheraton from reaping the reward of his talents? His designs were widely adopted during his lifetime. He says himself that his book was "recommended by many workmen of the first abilities in London, who have themselves inspected the work," and yet all his life he lacked the barest necessities of existence. The abundance and character of his work show that he was not lazy or vulgar. One cannot say that he was too much of an idealist or dreamer, because his furniture combines beauty with the utmost practicability. He probably lacked the business sense—the ability to "put it over" for his own benefit. Well, he is not the first genius whose grave is heaped in bay leaves.

In his last years, Sheraton, like Duncan Phyfe, was forced to follow the public demand for furniture in the Empire taste, and his later designs were so debased by the French influence that it seems almost unfair even to mention them. Like Duncan Phyfe, he loudly lamented this "foolish staring after French fashions" and deplored the fact that "a clumsy, four-footed stool from France will be admired by our Connoisseurs in preference to a first-rate cabinet of English production."

Under the headings of "Chairs" and "Tables" and "Sideboards" we have tried to make clear the outstanding characteristics of Sheraton's style. Study them carefully, for not only in some of the rarest and most beautiful old furniture in the world, but in thousands of pieces turned out by our factories to-day, you will find, tucked away somewhere, a touch of that saving grace we call the "Sheraton influence."

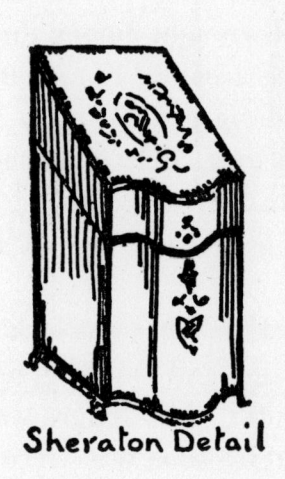

Sheraton Detail

ANTIQUES

SOFAS and SETTEES ought really to begin the other way around, for settees antedate sofas and, for that matter, settles antedate settees. They are all long seats meant to accommodate two people or, if you can't get rid of them, more than two. Fortunately a great deal that has been said about chairs applies equally well to sofas and settees, for they were made, of course, more or less to match the chairs.

Pine Settle

Settee with Turkey-work

SETTLE—The early form of long seat that afterward developed into the settee. Those made by our Pilgrim fathers were extremely simple in construction, being made with a very high back of plain lengthwise boards. A board at the sides from the top to the floor was shaped to form "wings" to keep off the draught, and the seat was low and narrow. Usually the top of the seat lifted up so that things could be stored in the space below—a space-saving arrangement in keeping with the gate-leg tables and "Presse" beds. Sometimes there was a little candle shelf attached to the back in the middle, but more often the iron candlestick was hooked or clamped to the side of the "wing." . . . In spite of their extreme simplicity—or perhaps because of it—these early settles are very appealing. One can so readily imagine them in front of the roaring fire, the light playing on the shy lovers who sit there hand in hand or upon the pale face and softly folded kerchief of her who "seeketh wool and flax, and worketh willingly with her hands."

SETTEE—By 1675 turned seats for two to match the chairs were made, and these were so much lighter than the clumsy settles, that they were called settees for short. Such rich pieces were often upholstered in Turkey-work to match the chairs and were found in houses where draughts were not so prevalent. In these same houses were found long couches for those who took their leisure in the day, a sort of chaise-longue with a chair back at one end. These usually had eight legs, and the legs and back were made in the manner of the time, Flemish, Dutch, or, when he came along, with Chippendale's ball-and-claw feet and fine chair back. . . . These cannot properly be called settees, however, but this is a good place to mention them.

CHIPPENDALE SETTEES—These were usually made the width of two seats and were either two open-work chair backs or upholstered all over like the easy chairs. Many handsome ones of both sorts are found here. They must, of course, have been brought over from England. One remarkably fine double chair with armchairs to match undoubtedly was, for it belonged to Governor John Wentworth, whose household goods were sold at auction by our new Federal Government in 1776. The backs are most elaborately and beautifully carved in the Chinese manner, the type of chair that Chippendale says is "suitable for a lady's boudoir and will likewise suit a Chinese temple"! The legs of this settee are, of course, square and straight. Others that have the typical carved splat back have the carved bandy legs with ball-and-claw feet. The seat is upholstered as a similar chair seat would be.

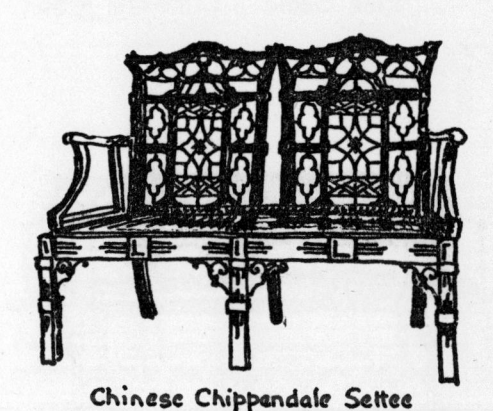

HEPPLEWHITE SETTEES—These were made in the same manner as Chippendale's; that is to say, two typical chair backs joined in one piece. Those that we find over here are very

Couch

Chinese Chippendale Settee

ANTIQUES

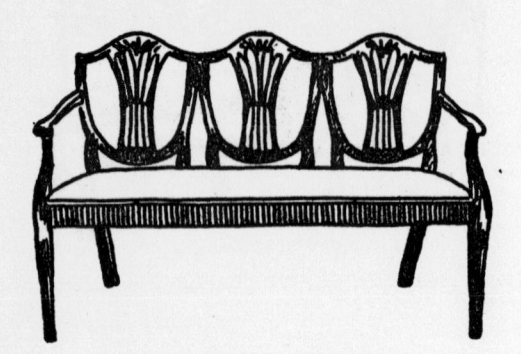

Hepplewhite Settee

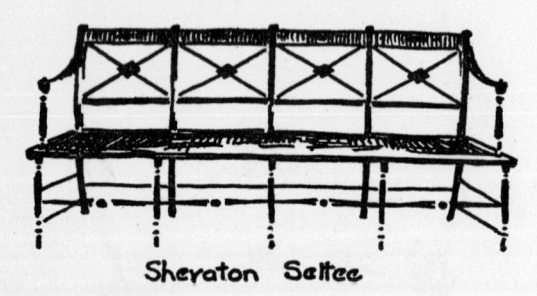

Sheraton Settee

lovely, the delicate shield-shaped backs, light structure, and tapering straight legs giving an appearance of great elegance. They are inlaid with fine lines and delicate designs, like the bellflower, and the seats are upholstered in fine brocade. Chairs, of course, were made to match them. We need not say that these were made about 1780.

SHERATON SETTEES, of course, surpass all others in airy grace combined with strength. They are usually longer than either Chippendale's or Hepplewhite's, combining three and even four chair backs. Some of them had fine cane seats and had cane in the backs, surrounded by the most delicate open woodwork inlaid and veneered or painted in dainty designs. This type of elegant and airy settee was enormously liked in America and many characteristic adaptations of it were made by our own workmen. As was usual when we made use of English designs, we simplified them greatly and put in something of our own, a certain simplicity and directness that make them very charming, at least to our eyes. We often find these long seats in the "Sheraton manner," three or four chairs long, with cane or rush or even solid wood seats and straight round legs. The backs are always open in some simple rendering of Sheraton's designs. They are painted and often decorated with stencilling of flowers. Just the same type, you see, as the "fancy" painted chairs of which the Hitchcock is a good example. They were made about 1800.

SHERATON SOFAS—Sofas are quite different from settees, being longer and entirely covered with upholstery;

that is to say, little wood shows except the legs and sometimes the arms and frame across the back. Those designed by Sheraton are the most liked, because of their simple elegance. They are usually slightly arched across the back, the arms coming down in a gentle curve tipping off into reeded pillars that continue down into the reeded legs. They usually have three or four small reeded legs in front without stretchers. The little woodwork that shows is either delicately carved or inlaid. They are covered in various fine stuffs.

EMPIRE SOFAS—The sofa was a very popular piece of furniture during the Empire period, perhaps because it was so big and took so much of the heavy ornamentation of the time. Sheraton's simple sofa soon gave way to curving lines and elaborate carving. Perhaps the most typical sofa of the Empire—at least here in America—was the elaborate "Cornucopia" of 1820-30. It is almost impossible to describe the convolutions of this sofa. The back was a series of swooping curves, sometimes with a straight piece across the middle, the arms curled over in a "horn of plenty," bursting with fruits and flowers, and the feet were usually lions' claws attached to flying wings spread out to support the seat. They were upholstered in velours or horsehair and under the curve of the cornucopia arms was stuffed a hard round cushion, called a "squab," to fill out the ridiculous waste of space at each end. . . . By the time Queen Victoria was in full swing, about 1850, the "Cornucopia" had given way to the thick pierced sort of Spanish-comb effect with which we are all only too familiar.

Sheraton Sofa

Empire Sofa

Victorian Sofa

ANTIQUES

SIDEBOARDS have no very long history, but what there is of it is most interesting. The sideboard is distinctly a modern piece of furniture. No such thing as the sideboard as we know it to-day had ever appeared until an English cabinet maker by the name of Thomas Shearer designed one for his book on furniture, published in 1788. Up to that time the cupboard had served to contain the china and foodstuffs, although there had been hints of the sideboard as early as 1750. Evidently Chippendale chose to ignore the hint, or perhaps he just simply missed it, for he contented himself with the sideboard table, which was merely a long serving table without drawers. Adam seems to have got the idea of a sideboard, for he added pedestals to match the side table, to stand at each end of it with urn-shaped boxes, one for ice water and one for hot, on top. These beautiful boxes, most delicately made of mahogany, with fine inlay, were soon utilized as knife boxes and fitted with little trays with openings in them through which the silver could be suspended. The pedestals were fitted with shelves for the care of plate or linen, the wine cooler stood under the serving table—and still no one thought of the sideboard. Then Shearer's design for a sideboard with drawers appeared. It didn't take Hepplewhite long to see the value of the idea, and when his book came out the following year it contained more and better sideboards. So did Sheraton's in 1791.

The sideboards of Hepplewhite and Sheraton are very similar, so much so that there is great difficulty in distinguishing between them. There are, however, one or two distinct points which, if we get them clearly in mind, will always come to our assistance. Hepplewhite—as usual—used the straight tapering leg, while Sheraton stuck pretty close to his reeded one. He also used the plain square one, but at least you may be sure the reeded one is NOT Hepplewhite. The great point of difference, however, is one that R. Davis Benn emphasizes in his excellent book on English furniture. He says that Hepplewhite "always employed the concave corner" and that Sheraton, on the contrary, "always has the convex corner." He seems pretty sure of it, too, for he puts it in italics and shows plates to prove it. The concave corners certainly gave Hepplewhite's sideboards the serpentine appearance that we know he liked so well.

HEPPLEWHITE SIDEBOARDS— Having fixed the corners firmly in mind we can describe the sideboards more fully, the description fitting both types except in such detail as we shall mention. The handsome pieces were usually about six feet long, twenty-eight inches wide, and forty inches high. They had the appearance of great lightness in spite of their size and the number of drawers and compartments they contained. Usually there were small drawers across the top with a cupboard in the centre below. On each side of the cupboard were two deep narrow drawers fitted with compartments for bottles. And on each end were the corner cupboards with the much-discussed convex or concave doors. This was the usual arrangement, but of course the space was divided in a dozen different ways. Sometimes the ends were square with the cupboards clear to the top. Sometimes the centre cupboard was omitted to give space for the wine cooler beneath. Two handsome knife boxes, not the urn-shape but the slant-top kind, stood on top at either end.

Hepplewhite Sideboard

SHERATON SIDEBOARDS—Sheraton, with his unerring sense of decoration combined with utility, often added a brass rail with a little "fulled-on" silk curtain, usually green, across the back against which to tilt the big pieces of silver, and fixed candlesticks at either end of it so that the light could shine down upon and enhance the beauty of the plate. The sideboards of both men were made in mahogany decorated with fine veneer and inlay. . . . Similar sideboards were made over here, more simply and often in maple, or in mahogany inlaid with maple, or in other combinations of

Sheraton Sideboard

native woods. Some of them were painted in designs to imitate inlay. All of them are very lovely. None of them were made after 1810.

EMPIRE SIDEBOARDS—After 1810 the same old heaviness began to creep in, and we find sideboards rapidly losing grace. They became very ponderous and square like the bureaus, dropping clear to the floor on short lions' or bears' feet. They lost all their curves —a heavy back-board took the place of Sheraton's delicate brass rail, and there were heavy carved columns up the corners and sometimes up the front. Of course, they gained much in roominess. They were made in mahogany, often veneered in the same wood of a lighter grain, or in the lugubrious black walnut that now began to come in vogue. They had many large brass mounts of the rosette and ring type, or plain wooden or glass knobs. We all know those great coffin-like black sideboards—and please do not call them Colonial.

MIXING TABLE AND CELLARET— Back in the good old days of 1776 hard drinking was the rule everywhere. Both in England and over here the cellaret under the sideboard was the proper thing. These were often made of mahogany and very handsome, sometimes bound with brass and lined with zinc to hold the ice-cooled wine. Mixing tables with compartments for bottles and the other necessities for making punch often accompanied the sideboard in the dining room. Would it be out of place, I wonder, to mention here that it is said that George Washington himself invented a little two-bottle coaster on wheels to help speed up the progress of the wine around the table?

SILVERWARE, in America, has a long, interesting, and honourable history beginning almost with the first settlement and continuing until modern manufacturing methods robbed it of individuality and consequently of interest.

It seems strange at first thought that there should have been silver of such high quality in the Colonies. This was a new country, not over-concerned with luxurious living, and one would think that silversmithing would be one of the last trades to flourish. But there were many prosperous merchants here gathering in coin from Spain, Holland, and Portugal, and it is no more than natural that from time to time they should want to gratify their pride by taking a parcel of it to the silversmith to be turned into plate.

But it was not done every day. When a man came in and thumped down a bag of coin on the counter it was a matter of importance, not only to him but to the silversmith, who more likely than not was a man of high standing in the community, holding public office or acting as banker with a reputation for piety and integrity to maintain. It was no light matter for such a man to stamp his name upon a piece of silver, for he knew that when it left his hands his reputation and his honour went with it. The amazingly high quality of the work that has come down to us shows how worthy these men were of the confidence placed in them.

The simplest way to go about the story of silver will be to explain first some of the early forms, many of which are no longer in use; then to say a word about how they were made; and after that give the histories of one or two of the great silversmiths that will be, at least in part, typical of them all.

BEAKERS are a very early and simple form of drinking cup. In mediæval times men drank from the drinking horn, and probably the first beaker was made when some inspired person thought of cutting off the end of the horn and fitting a bottom to it. At any rate, that is the shape of the beaker, smaller at the bottom than at the top, flaring a little at the lip and setting down flat or on a slight moulding. Silver beakers were made both in New England and New Amsterdam from about 1660 until the end of the 18th Century. The

ANTIQUES

early ones, especially those from New England, were often plain and depended entirely upon their line for beauty.

TANKARDS are another early form of drinking vessel, and generally speaking, are just the reverse of the beaker; that is, they are broader at the bottom than at the top. The English ones that served as models for our earliest ones were cylindrical and broad with a heavy flat hinged lid, a thick scroll handle, and a moulded base. Later on, about 1750, when cabriole legs and curves were fashionable, the tankard became bulbous and "toby" shaped. These, too, were usually plain, depending on the moulded borders, the thumb-piece, and handle ornaments for decoration. Most pieces of silver were engraved with the coat of arms of the owner, or had his initials about them somewhere.

MUGS are no more than small tankards, with the handle but without the lid.

CAUDLE CUPS—During the 17th Century hot drinks were much in favour in England. Caudle was one of these drinks, and was made of thin gruel, mixed with wine, sweetened and spiced. One cannot imagine anything more awful to drink, except, perhaps, posset, which was very like caudle only made with milk. Deep gourd-shaped silver cups with two handles and sometimes a lid were made for these drinks, and are among the loveliest of early silver cups. These were made in the Colonies in the late 17th and early 18th centuries, but after tea and coffee drinking became general, about 1730, caudle and caudle cups went out of fashion.

PORRINGERS are an ancient dish, shallow enough for solid food, deep enough for liquid. The mediæval European ones were made of wood or pewter or silver or even gold, decorated with jewels. These usually had two handles. Those made in England were smaller and had only one handle, and were most unpleasantly called "bleeding cups" because surgeons used them. Over here in America we made ours with only one handle, but larger, and they were a most important dish in every household. Usually they were made of pewter, with an occasional handsome silver one, and hung in rows along the dresser shelves. The handles stuck out flat from the lip of the dish and were pierced, the early ones from 1660 to 1700 showing the heart-shape piercing also used in the chair splats at that time. The "keyhole" handle found on most Colonial porringers came in about 1725, many of them bearing the initials of both husband and wife in crude block letters. The porringer continued in use until porcelain took the place of metal for table ware.

TEA- AND COFFEE-POTS—Tea and coffee drinking became very popular about 1700, and silver pots modelled after the little Chinese china ones were made. At first they were alike for both beverages and very small, because of the scarcity of both commodities, but as importations grew larger the pots grew larger, too, especially those for coffee—just as they are to-day. Cream was not used in tea until the 18th Century, so we do not find cream pots and sugar bowls with the very early pots, but by the time the classic influence of Adam swept over England in 1760 they were being made and we find silver following the mode with lovely urn-shaped tea- and coffee-pots, hot-water kettles, sugar bowls, and helmet pitchers.

CHOCOLATE-POTS were very like the coffee-pots except that they were apt to be somewhat bigger and more ornate, and they had a hole in the lid through which the thick substance could be stirred.

SPOONS are the cause of great agitation to collectors of old silver who study their changes of form with scrupulous attention—the shape of each bowl and handle, the way they are joined, and the markings and decorations—but, much as we should like to, we have no place for that here. The earliest spoons were hammered out of one piece of metal and were strong as spades, but by the time the Colonists got to making silver, spoons were made in two parts, the handle and bowl being joined together by a long tongue down the under-

ANTIQUES

side of the bowl. An early and popular spoon thus joined is known as the "rat-tail" and was made about 1725. The tail became a faint line by the middle of the century. The bowls developed from a blunt egg shape to the long, shallow-pointed bowl attached to the fiddle-back handle—a spoon with which we are all familiar.

Other shapes were made in silver—beautiful bowls, brasiers, alms basins, strainers, salts, shoe-buckles, tongs, etc., all most lovely and interesting to study, and priceless to possess. We will try now to give some little idea of how these pieces were made.

HOW EARLY SILVER WAS MADE—One of the reasons why early silver is so lovely is because it was made piece by piece, each piece the work of one man who watched over every step in its development from the moment he weighed out the coin and decided what could be done with it, until he held the finished vessel on the palm of his hand for one last critical study. He put something of himself into it—something of his honour and his pride and his intelligence—which remains visible in it forever.

After he had received the coins of various kinds and qualities, he melted them up and refined them to the proper standard. In England the standard then, as now, was 925 parts pure, that is, 11 oz. 2 Dwts. pure silver and 18 Dwts. of alloy in every 12 oz. This is called "sterling" silver. Every piece of silverware made over there was required to be of that quality, and was inspected and "hall-marked" at the Goldsmith's Hall in the district in which it was made. That is why we find as many as four "hall-marks" on English silver—the stamp of the Guild, the government stamp, the maker's mark, and the date. We never have had such a trade guild over here, but after the beginning of the 19th Century the word "coin" was stamped on silver to denote the quality, and after 1865 we adopted the English "sterling."

But having no guild to inspect his work was all the more reason for the Colonial silversmith to watch with scrupulous care the refining of his silver. This he did by repeatedly testing a bit of the molten mass on a "touch stone" with silver known to be of proper quality. When it reached standard he ran it off into a shallow pan and allowed it to cool. The rectangular block thus formed was then rolled or beaten out into a sheet of the required thinness. Experts can tell much about when and where early silver was made by the thickness of the sheet, pieces made in New Amsterdam, for instance, being much heavier than those made in New England.

While he was beating it, the silversmith had frequently to reheat the silver to keep it from becoming brittle, and this left a faint, dark, pearly tinge, called a "fire-skin," on the surface of the metal, never found in modern "buffed" silver. After the sheet had reached a proper thinness the master took a pair of shears, cut out a circular piece, and laid it over a mould of the shape he desired to make. Then with sure clean blows he beat the silver to fit the mould. One can easily imagine a bowl, for example, being made in this way. This was called "lifting" the silver. The blows of the hammer, faintly visible on old silver, left a surface of great beauty, mellow and soft, with a lustre impossible to obtain in any other way. So-called "beaten silver" is made to-day, but is in no way comparable with the old ware.

After the master had shaped his vessel into lines that satisfied his critical sense of proportion, he proceeded to decorate it, and it was here that his ability was put to the test. Many and many a time, with rare judgment, he let the sheer beauty of outline speak for itself, and these undecorated pieces are, perhaps, the most exquisite. Or he may have added just a simple moulding about the base or the rim. His handles were usually a simple strap bent into a scroll with a bit of moulded ornament at the tip and thumb piece. If he wished to enrich it still more he added a band of fluting or other simple design in repoussé work, an effective decoration made by pushing (repoussé) the design out from the inside with tools made for that purpose. Or he applied a design in cut-card work, a sort of stencil pattern cut from the sheet silver. Perhaps he used chasing, which was denting the design into the piece by means of a blunt instrument struck with a mallet; quite a different process from engraving, where the surface was cut away with a sharp tool. And he used piercing for such objects as brasiers and strainers, and for the handles of porringers.

It was his employment of these means of decoration, sometimes several of them on one piece, that marked the master. Over-ornamentation, meaningless design, decoration applied to cover up defects, are never found in the work of great men, and it is astonishing how many pieces of silver, the work of many men over a period of many years, have come down to us that are classic in perfection of workmanship. If all of them had been the work of one great man, a later Cellini, it would have been remarkable enough, but that there should have been at least twenty men working between the years 1660 and 1800 who should have turned out work of this description is extraordinary. It would be a pleasure if we could talk about each one of them, for each in his own way was interesting, his life wrapped up in the history of our country, but we can take only two, the first and the last, each typical of his time and of his fellow craftsmen.*

JOHN HULL was the first, and one of the greatest, of the New England silversmiths. He came to Boston in 1635 when he was eleven years old and soon after learned the trade of silversmithing. In 1652 he became Mint Master, and with his partner, Robert Sanderson, a skilled craftsman who had practised his trade in England before coming to America, he coined the famous "pine tree shilling," the first money coined in what is now the United States. He remained Mint Master for thirty years, became treasurer for the Colony, a founder of the Old South Church, and a wealthy and influential citizen. He was a man of great piety and classic learning, a worthy founder of the long line of early American silversmiths who followed the high traditions laid down by him.

PAUL REVERE—And now we come to the story of Paul Revere, not the "midnight" one, for that was a mere incident in the life of this versatile, energetic, and extraordinary man, but to the much more exciting and romantic story of his life.

Strange as it may seem, Paul of the famous midnight ride was a silversmith. His father had been born in France of Huguenot parents and christened

---

*The above information as to the manufacture of early silver was obtained from Miss C. Louise Avery's excellent book, "American Silver of the XVII and XVIII Centuries."

Apollos Revoire. He learned the trade of silversmithing in Europe, came to Boston in 1723, anglicized his name to Paul Revere, prospered, married, and had twelve children, of whom the third, Paul, Jr., was destined to become the most famous of New England silversmiths.

The boy was born in Boston in 1735. While he was still a lad he learned his trade from his father and showed great talent, not only in designing silver but in chasing and engraving. When he was nineteen his father died and young Paul took charge of the shop. How he managed to do the beautiful work we know to be his, painstaking and delicate, it is hard to say, for he was of fiery disposition and an ardent patriot mixed up in all the rebellion that kept Boston stirred up for years before the Revolution.

In 1757 he married Sarah Orne who died in 1773 after bearing him eight children. Five months later Paul married again. That same year he took part in the Boston Tea Party and rode as a messenger for the Committee of Safety to New York and Philadelphia, trying to stir up coöperation there, once carrying the "Suffolk Resolves," the forerunner of the Declaration of Independence. The following year, 1774, he rode to Portsmouth, N. H., with news which resulted in the New Hampshire Sons of Liberty surprising the fort there, the first armed resistance to British rule. The next April, 1775, saw the famous ride to Lexington which must have seemed a mere jaunt to the indefatigable Paul, who by this time was a vigorous man of forty, accustomed to hazards and excitement. He was twice captured and twice escaped as he rode through the night, rousing the Minute Men with the news that flew through every Middlesex village and town. That ride was the opening act to the greatest day in the history of our country, the preface to the "shot heard 'round the world."

> Listen, my children, and you shall hear
> Of the midnight ride of Paul Revere

will send a thrill up the spine of every little boy and girl as long as the Stars and Stripes float over the Fourth Grade, but few of them will know that Paul was a silversmith.

During the Revolution Paul Revere made gun-powder and mended cannon, saw service in both Massachusetts and Rhode Island, and was in command of the fort at Castle William. In 1779 he took part in the ill-timed expedition to Maine during which he was charged with insubordination and arrested. After his release he fought for two years until the charge was withdrawn and his reputation entirely cleared.

After the war Revere returned to Boston and went back seriously to his trade. In 1783 he opened a shop where, besides the silverware made there, he sold jewellery. In 1794 he started an iron and brass foundry where, with his son Joseph, he began casting church bells, cannon, and the metal fittings for ships. This was the first concern in America to smelt and refine copper ore, and they were very successful at it. Paul Revere continued active at his trade of silversmithing and in his various enterprises until he died, a prosperous and honoured man, at his home in Boston in the year 1818.

It seems extraordinary that a man of his temperament, virile and active, should have executed the many and exquisite pieces of silverware that reflect a strong artistic feeling and rare creative ability—work that unquestionably meant hours of the utmost patience and concentration. Paul Revere was a man apparently of wide extremes, and they are nowhere more strikingly illustrated than in his greatest piece of work—a large punch bowl wrought for the "Sons of Liberty"—the finest piece of silverware in this country.

Colonial Silver

- Porringer Vernon 1700
- Beaker by Hull 1650
- Tankard 1750
- Caster 1725
- Ladle 1760
- J. Noyes Fork 1750
- Punch-Bowl by Paul Revere
- Coffee-Pot 1790

T

And make it plain upon tables, that he may run who readeth it.

OLD TESTAMENT.

TABLES come pretty close to being as varied and interesting as chairs—and as difficult to classify. They have no such helpful and distinguishing feature as "backs" to aid us. The top will not help us much, for square, round, rectangular, or oval tops appear on tables of all times and types. This time we shall have to concentrate our attention on the legs, and fortunately all that we have said about chair legs is true of table legs as well. We will get at the tables just as we did the chairs—by dividing them into two groups: the early Colonial tables and those that sprang from the designs of the "Big Four."

"TABLE BORDS" were the earliest type of table used in this country and they had been used for centuries in Europe. They were no more than a board laid upon trestles, just as we improvise a table to-day when we go camping. When the meal was over the board and trestles were put aside, leaving the room free. "Table bords" are mentioned in the earliest inventories, and we have examples in museums.

TRESTLE TABLES are the direct development from the "table bord" with the top fastened down permanently to the trestles and with a stout stretcher running from end to end through the middle of them about six inches from the floor. This was to put the feet on, to keep them off the cold and dirty floor. Such tables are crude and extremely rare, for the long narrow type of table was on the wane in Europe when the Pilgrims came over here. Smaller tables with four legs

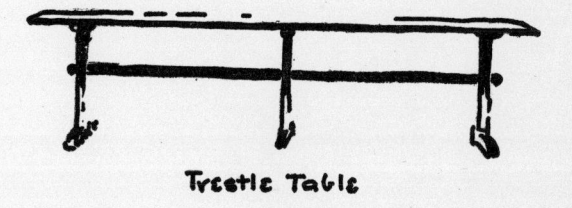

Trestle Table

Chair Table

instead of trestles are far more typical of the home. Trestle tables were used in taverns, and people sat at them on "forms" or benches.

REFECTORY TABLE is not at all a Colonial table, but we may as well explain its type while we are here. It is a long narrow table on legs instead of trestles, six of them usually, with a heavy stretcher all around instead of through the middle. It is called "refectory" from the fact that it is the type of table used in the refectory or dining hall in early monasteries. In Jacobean times they were handsome huge tables with enormous bulbous legs. But you remember that ponderous heavy stuff was beginning to go out when our forefathers came over here. Some of it was brought over before 1700, the "Presse" cupboards with the same bulbous uprights at the corners, and the great wainscot chairs, but I doubt if any of these big tables came. They may have come. So may the great beds that matched them, but if they did we have no trace of them. . . . We did have a table over here, however, that probably was inspired by memories of the old "refectory" at home. This was a small rectangular table with four stout turned legs and a heavy straight stretcher all around. Sometimes it had a drawer, and sometimes the "apron" or frame at the top which joined the legs was nicely shaped. They were made of oak or maple. Sometimes the top was pine. They were simple tables but full of charm. Similar strong joined stools were made to use with them. They were made about 1690 and are typically American.

CHAIR TABLES—Another early form, inventoried about 1644. A sort of space-saving utility piece having a round top attached to the frame which, when the top was tipped up against the wall, could be used as a chair. To add further to its usefulness, there was a drawer in the chair frame. Interesting but not particularly attractive either as a table or a chair.

GATE-LEG TABLE—This graceful and useful table, the first to have the drop-leaf, came into use about 1700 and with slight variations has been with us ever since. It was this table that put the old refectory out of the picture. It was light, it saved space, it was attractive and full of charm. No wonder it served for many years as a general utility table. When its leaves were expanded it was generally round or oval—a pleasant change from the long narrow board—and would comfortably seat eight people, or even ten. In its smaller forms it served as a card or tea table. Tea and coffee drinking, by the way, had become enormously popular by 1700, and this social habit was largely responsible for the great numbers of small tables that were now made. The earliest gate-legs were made with turned legs and stout stretchers, and some of them had so many legs they were called "hundred-legged"—and looked it. Most of them, however, had only four pairs—two stationary and two that spread out to support the leaves. Some of them were so narrow when folded that they could not stand alone and had to be tilted against the wall. . . . About 1725 the gate-leg was made with the Dutch cabriole leg and stubby feet. They must have been very popular and well made, for they are still to be found in good condition and are particularly

Gate-Leg Table

Dutch Table

delightful when made in maple. . . . By 1750 the gate-leg was made in mahogany with ball-and-claw feet, and this, too, is a delightful table. Once in a great while you see an early gate-leg with several slender spindle legs—the "spider-leg" type that is so much copied for tea tables to-day—but these are very rare, as are all slender pieces of that period.

BUTTERFLY TABLE—The most endearing of all early tables, and made about 1700, the same time as the gate-leg and a sort of variation of it. While gate-legs were often large, to seat eight or ten people, the butterfly was always small, sometimes not more than twenty inches from the floor. They are the drop-leaf type of table with outward "raked" turned legs and plain or turned stretchers. Graceful wing-shaped brackets, from which they get their name, are set into the stretchers and swing forward on each side to support the little leaves. These tables were often made in maple, and anything more alluring to the lover of the antique than this quaint little piece cannot be imagined. They seem to have originated in Connecticut. At any rate, the Butterfly is our very own table, with no inspiration but Yankee ingenuity behind it.

OTHER EARLY TABLES—Hosts of small tables were made from 1700 on. Stands are spoken of as early as 1675. The tops were round, square, or oval, the simple turned pillar supported on a plain cross-piece or on three spreading feet—the forerunner of the tripod table so beautifully developed by Chippendale, as we shall see in just a moment. Tea tables were oblong with slim cabriole legs. Sometimes they had a raised rim. Sometimes there were little slides at each end for the candlesticks. Small plain tables with shallow drawers were used as work tables. The small stout turned tables continued to be made.

That covers what may be called the typical early American tables, made in native woods by native workmen for simple home use. All of them are very much cherished to-day, and as they were made of sound maple, cherry, oak, or pine with ash, hickory, apple-wood, and other handy woods combined to give them strength, they may still be found, after years of hard service, in as good condition as on the day they were made. We shall now go on to the more delicate and elegant pieces that were imported from England or made over here after the designs of the "Big Four." It is true of tables, as it was true of chairs, that those made in America were simpler than their English prototypes.

CHIPPENDALE TRIPOD — Perhaps the most typical and certainly the most interesting Chippendale table is the round tiptop tripod tea table. Chippendale made so much of this table and developed it so beautifully that he is often credited with originating it. As a matter of fact, he came so close to it that we may safely say that all tables of this description belong to the Chippendale period. . . . In general, they were all alike, made of mahogany, the round top cut from the solid wood and mounted on a tiny turn-table so that they would revolve and, when released by a spring, tip up to set close to the wall when not in use. The turn-table was attached to a pillar base which was supported by three out-springing cabriole legs resting on ball-and-claw feet. That was their basic appearance, but Chippendale, with the same wealth of imagination that he displayed in his chair backs, developed them in endless variety. . . . The earliest and simplest of them—

Dish-Top

Pie-crust

Pierced Table

Scallop Edge

about 1750—we call the "Dish Top" because of the simple rim around the top to keep the dishes from falling off. It had a plain turned pillar and no carving except on the ball-and-claw feet. It was in the carving of the rim and upon the pillar and legs and feet that Chippendale elaborated the table. The legs and feet display the same delicate designs that we find on the chair legs, and much of the beauty in these tables depends on the niceness of proportion in the spread of the legs. The pillar was often reeded and the turnings carved. But it is the carving of the rim around the top that most fascinates us. This took many forms, the most popular and delicate being the irregular "Pie crust" pattern. They were also carved in regular, rather deep scallops and occasionally in long scrolls. Later ones show an openwork pierced rim like the mahogany trays of that time. . . . Smaller taller stands of a similar kind were made to hold the candlesticks, and there were tiny ones for the teakettle, to accompany the bigger tea table. All of these tripod tables were made continuously and in great variety from 1750 to 1775, when with the appearance of the designs of Hepplewhite and Sheraton they were put aside for tables with straight lines.

CHIPPENDALE'S CARD TABLES—Another characteristic Chippendale table is the card table. Gaming at this time was a most popular diversion in both England and America, and card tables were made in great numbers. The kind most commonly used had the cabriole leg with ball-and-claw foot and the top divided to fold over upon itself when not in use. When the top was open it was usually covered with cloth stretched tight over the wood. The four corners were dished to hold the candlesticks, and there were four oval-shaped cups in the edge for money or counters. Those made by Chippendale were elaborately carved about the knees and feet, and the tops were sometimes shaped in deep curves with more carving around the lower edge of the apron. Card tables were also made quite plain, with straight square legs and a plain flap-over top. . . . There were similar tables made for drawing with adjustable tops to hold the drawing board.

OTHER TABLES—We have spoken of Chippendale's sideboard table for the dining room. He also made great numbers of oblong tables for use against the wall, many of them, especially those made in the Chinese manner, extremely elaborate, being loaded down with carving and pierced fretwork. These were used to hold the curios and small *objets d'art* so popular in those days, and they usually had a fretwork gallery around the top to keep these things from falling off. Most tables of this type had the square leg but, of course, they appear in great variety with the cabriole leg as well. He also made tea tables with four legs, as well as the tripod type, the tops, with carved or fretted rims, being detachable to serve as trays. The Chippendale dining table was the round or oval mahogany drop-leaf with the ball-and-claw feet.

Chippendale Card-Table

Chinese Fret-Work Table

To say that we have covered Chippendale tables would be nonsense. Tables, even more than chairs, are individuals. Chairs were made in groups or sets, and we can more or less generalize about them, but tables were made one by one, and to be thoroughly known, must be studied that way. However, we can depend upon the tripod, the flat-top bandy-legged gaming table, and the square-legged over-ornamented fretwork table being Chippendale.

Hepplewhite Dining Table

Console Table

HEPPLEWHITE AND SHERATON TABLES—As we know so well by this time, these two men, backed by Adam, completely revolutionized the character of house furnishings, changing them almost overnight from the old fashions that had slowly developed through the centuries into something new—the furniture of modern times. Nothing could be in sharper contrast to old Chippendale's heavy mahogany and elaborate carving than their light and graceful designs, particularly those for tables. Both designers made tables in great variety, large and small. They were always graceful and airily poised, more often than not in light woods like satin-wood, highly finished and elaborately decorated with inlay or painting. Carving was delicate and discreetly placed when used at all, and while, of course, they both worked in mahogany, it is not characteristic of them as it is of Chippendale and Phyfe. . . . Both of them brought out new designs for tables, among them the

EXTENSION DINING TABLE—This table seems properly to belong to Hepplewhite. At any rate, his designs antedate those of Sheraton by two short years, so we will give him credit for it. It was of great importance and soon developed into a table of rare dignity and beauty. It was made in several separate parts, which could be fitted together making a table of any desired length, the end sections being semi-circular and with a drop-leaf on the other side. . . . The legs were slender, straight, and tapering, the wood, of course, being mahogany. Sheraton's extension table was very similar except that he used his favourite round and reeded leg.

PIER OR CONSOLE TABLES—Hepplewhite was fond of these small tables and says in his book that "they are becoming an article of much fashion." They were made semi-circular in front, straight across the back to set against the wall between windows or with a mirror above them. Not being for general use they admit, as he says, of much elegance and ornament, and he made the most of the opportunity, developing them in mahogany richly inlaid with satin-wood and other contrasting woods, or in light woods delicately painted with the bellflower, etc. That type of painted or richly inlaid table with delicate straight legs set into the curved front is particularly typical of Hepplewhite.

CARD AND TEA TABLES were very like the pier tables except that they had a fold-over top that rested flat on the companion half or up against the wall when not in use. These lovely tables have always been extremely popular here in America, and were imported or made here in great numbers. Those made over here were not nearly so elaborate as the English ones and were often inlaid or combined with curly maple, which the English never were. . . . Sheraton's tables of this type were very similar except that here, too, he used the round reeded leg, and very often the edge of the table was reeded horizontally. . . . His leaves, too, were more apt to be square with the corners shaped or the edges serpentine. . . . Flap-top tables that are called "late Sheraton," about 1810, verging on the Empire, have much heavier reeded legs and the serpentine curves very pronounced.

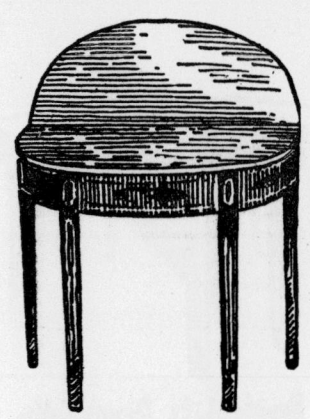

Hepplewhite Card-Table

Sheraton Card-Table

Pembroke Table

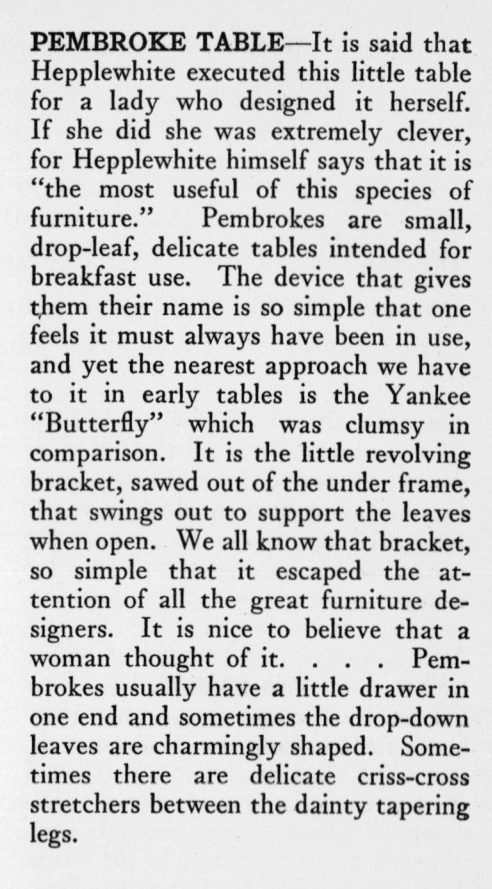

PEMBROKE TABLE—It is said that Hepplewhite executed this little table for a lady who designed it herself. If she did she was extremely clever, for Hepplewhite himself says that it is "the most useful of this species of furniture." Pembrokes are small, drop-leaf, delicate tables intended for breakfast use. The device that gives them their name is so simple that one feels it must always have been in use, and yet the nearest approach we have to it in early tables is the Yankee "Butterfly" which was clumsy in comparison. It is the little revolving bracket, sawed out of the under frame, that swings out to support the leaves when open. We all know that bracket, so simple that it escaped the attention of all the great furniture designers. It is nice to believe that a woman thought of it. . . . Pembrokes usually have a little drawer in one end and sometimes the drop-down leaves are charmingly shaped. Sometimes there are delicate criss-cross stretchers between the dainty tapering legs.

Sofa Table

SOFA TABLES were made by both Hepplewhite and Sheraton, those of the latter being particularly lovely. They were oblong tables with a small drop leaf at each end, and with end supports connected by a stretcher. They usually had two shallow drawers, one that pulled out on one side and one on the other. They were often made of satin-wood exquisitely inlaid, and were meant to use beside a sofa, as the name implies. They are a particularly lovely drawing-room table, and have recently come into great vogue again as writing tables.

Most of the descriptions so far will apply to Sheraton tables as well as those of Hepplewhite, if we keep in mind Sheraton's preference for the round reeded leg and the fact that he used inlay much more extensively than painting. Also that his designs were apt to be more graceful and perfect in proportion than Hepplewhite's, who sometimes made mistakes. Sheraton never did. His work was always harmonious and perfect in every detail, and he showed far more inventiveness in design. In fact, he designed any number of small "trick" tables that concealed all sorts of devices.

SHERATON "KIDNEY" TABLE— Sheraton himself named this table because "it resembles in form that intestine part of animals so called." It was originally an "inventive" piece of furniture having an adjustable rising flap to answer the requirements of writing, reading, or drawing. When closed, Sheraton says, it occupies a small space and is a dainty occasional table. This tiny table of delightful shape was afterward made without the inventive part, quite simply as an occasional table and a most charming one it is, too. The "kidney" desk table, bowed comfortably about the knees of the writer and with tiers of drawers to the floor, also sprang from that same design.

Kidney Table

SHERATON WORK TABLES—While Hepplewhite made dainty work tables, we must give Sheraton credit for the loveliest ones. They were square or octagonal in shape, with two shallow drawers, the top one sometimes fitted with tiny compartments for spools and sewing materials. The legs were usually reeded, tapering to the floor to a size hardly larger than a ten-cent piece. The tops of the legs, delicately carved or turned, extended along the piece to the top where they formed little round corners. To a delicate

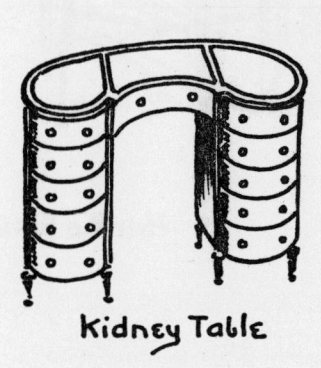

Sheraton Work-Table

wooden frame that slid forward or out from the side beneath the drawers was attached a chintz or pleated silk work-bag. It is impossible to exaggerate the usefulness and charm of these delightful tables—or possibly I am over-enthusiastic because I have one that was made in Boston in 1810 and stood in the same cool high-panelled room all those years until it came to me. Mine is all mahogany, but many of those made over here have curly maple inlaid in the drawers. After the Empire influence began to creep in about 1815 the dainty reeded legs became coarser and carved with acanthus design, and it is not fair, after that, to call these tables "Sheraton."

Martha Washington

MARTHA WASHINGTON WORK TABLE—There is a most useful and much disputed work table which is called the "Martha Washington." This table does not appear in England or in the books of either Hepplewhite or Sheraton. If Martha Washington really owned one it must have been made over here. I am inclined to think it is a modern adaptation combining the good features of several old types.

These tables cover most of the types that were brought over or made here from the designs of Hepplewhite or Sheraton. As in the case of Chippendale, we leave them with reluctance, feeling that scant justice has been done to a subject rich in variety, but we must get on to the tables made in America by Duncan Phyfe.

Phyfe, you remember, like Chippendale, worked almost entirely in mahogany with carving for decoration. There, however, the resemblance stops, for in design Phyfe followed Sheraton and Adam, in so far as he followed any one. He made tables that show the influence of both masters but in each case gave the piece a decided turn of his own.

PHYFE DINING TABLES—One of the most beautiful and important tables made by Phyfe was his dining table, not the early one with the reeded legs, rounded ends, and drop leaves almost exactly like Sheraton's, but the one that many people regard as the most beautiful dining table ever made. It was extended by putting in extra leaves instead of tables, and could be pulled out to great length. These tables were supported on pedestal bases which in turn rested upon the long down-swinging graceful legs for which Phyfe is so justly famous. The legs were often delicately carved with Phyfe's favourite leaf design or with rows of delicate reeding and usually ended in fine brass mounts with castors. Reeding often accentuated the beautiful sweep of the edge of the table.

CARD TABLES—Very like Sheraton's with the flap-over leaf that rested against the wall, except that these tables, too, were mounted on pedestals with the down-swinging legs sweeping out from them. The designs of Phyfe's table pedestals are varied. Sometimes they are no more than a simply turned and nicely carved post, sometimes there are four smaller carved posts grouped together, most often they are the delightful and characteristic lyre design —sometimes *two* lyres crossed. The strings on these are brass or whalebone. All of these pedestals occur on card tables. Phyfe also used the lyre motif on the ends of sofa tables.

WORK TABLES—Phyfe's work tables are all very like Sheraton's, with the reeded legs, tiny drawers, and silk workbag on a sliding frame. Some of them have semicircular or octagonal extensions at the side with the little flat tops.

Phyfe Dining Table

Phyfe Card-Table

ANTIQUES

You will remember that the Empire influence came in just in time to torment both Sheraton and Phyfe and to cause much disaster in their designs. . . . We will see what the Empire did to tables before we leave them with a sigh, of both relief and regret.

Pillar & Claw Dining Table

Empire Work Table

PILLAR - AND - CLAW DINING TABLE—This great clumsy heavy thing shows what happened under the Empire influence to Phyfe's delicate extension table with the pedestal supports and lovely legs. Now the pedestal has become as massive as a tree; it is covered with coarse carving, and the delicate reeded legs have turned to out-springing lions' legs and claws, carved to look as beastly as possible. For some reason or other this pillar-and-claw pedestal was extremely popular from about 1810 clear up to Victoria's time. It appeared on everything—centre tables, piano stools, piano legs, everywhere where an excuse could be found to use it. It was that sort of thing that Phyfe fought so desperately against—and failed to check.

WORK TABLES—The Empire work tables weren't so bad. Those that followed Sheraton and Phyfe became heavy, of course; the legs were carved with ubiquitous spiral acanthus designs, the drawers became more numerous and bigger and the whole thing lost grace; but the tables were nice. Some of them were set up on heavy urn-shaped pedestals with four stout legs. Sometimes these were in curly maple or had curly maple drawers which went far to redeem them. Still another type that we may call Empire was mounted on a plain round pillar or urn-shaped post which rested on a solid square base with four curl-overs at the corners for feet. That is a late and very common type of work table. We can all remember one or two of them in our own homes.

V

"Gentlemen—The QUEEN!"

VICTORIAN—We remember saying that "Empire was the last of the so-called period styles in furniture." How could we! How could Victoria have slipped our mind, for if any one ever had an era, clear, clean-cut, never-to-be-forgotten, it was that good queen. She ascended the throne of England, a girl of eighteen, in 1837 and never budged from it for sixty-four years. During all that time she guided her people with steady, shrewd intelligence, gaining and deserving the unswerving devotion that welded together the millions of souls throughout her far-flung empire. A great and good queen. One cannot say enough in admiration of Victoria, but, oh, her furniture!

Perhaps it isn't fair to blame Victoria for the furniture of her time, but at any rate she didn't chop off the heads of the people who made it, which unquestionably was an oversight. But remember that the world had a good start on the downward path, owing to the Empire influence, and perhaps she couldn't stop it. At any rate, we will leave her out of what we have to say about Victorian furniture.

Very little has been written about the furniture of the Victorian era. Perhaps it touches us too nearly. Perhaps we hesitate to tackle that nightmare of black walnut, wax-work, hair ornaments, and gilded rolling pins. I am not going to say much about it myself except by way of example, lest we, too—and how near we come to it at times—should dally on the middle path trying to be "useful as well as ornamental" and failing in both. That, I think, was behind the Victorian muddle. What else can explain, for instance, a clock in the middle of the tummy of the Venus de Milo? Or salad served in Calla lilies? It explains the "tidies" that were meant to protect and didn't protect, that were meant to be beautiful and were hideous. It explains the coy bunch of daisies on the coal scuttle and the incredible ornaments made from the hair of the dear departed. Read, for example, this advertisement in the *Ladies' Companion* of 1850:

This work [hair work] has now become a drawing room occupation as elegant and free from all annoyance of litter, dirt and unpleasant smells as the much practised netting, knitting and crochetting can be, while a small handkerchief will at any time cover the apparatus and materials in use. . . . Ladies will be themselves enabled to manufacture the hair of beloved friends into bracelets, chains, rings and ear-rings, and thus ensure that they do actually wear the memento they prize and not a fabric substituted for it, as we fear has sometimes been the case.

What, except for utter confusion of values, could explain a drawing-room occupation like that! These beings wanted to be practical but lacked the clear, direct vision of people who must actually be practical through necessity, as the Pilgrims were, and which resulted in their arriving at Beauty by an indirect route. They wanted to be "artistic" but shirked the grim, hard road that leads to Art. They were too well fed and prosperous, too smug to work, and so they dabbled, covering their weakness under a heavy wash of sentimentality. It isn't that they knew no better. The same stock, not two generations before, had produced Chippendale, Adam, and Sheraton. They simply didn't or wouldn't face the music. They let themselves be carried along by fads, and as there is no truth in fads, the whole fabric of their lives became artificial. It was an era of the great god Sham.

But the fat, pompous, conceited old dears of the Victorian era were not the first to sell their birthright for a mess of pottage, nor will they be the last. It will always be easier to go down hill than up, to follow the crowd than to resist it. It takes courage to see Beauty where other eyes have failed, for to have a vision of the nymph you must stand alone, you must think for yourself —and that, sometimes, is more than mere mortals have the courage to do.

W

The broad-axe to the gnarlèd oak,
The mallet to the pin!
—W<small>HITTIER</small>: "The Ship Builder."

WOODS—It is never pleasant to think about cutting down trees. Those dull, sinister blows echoing through the silent forest are not nice to hear, but if trees must come down it is some consolation to know that the best of them, the noblest and straightest, get into the hands of cabinet makers who treat them with respect, often with tenderness, as Phyfe did, trying their utmost to bring out their full beauty in forms of furniture, and that in those forms they came into our homes where we love and care for them. The kind of people who love trees will love furniture, especially old furniture, so perhaps Fate is not unkind to trees. They are not changed in the twinkling of an eye, but who knows that they do not find new life in their new forms?

It is a good thing, in looking at furniture, to know what kind of wood the piece is made of, not only for practical purposes, but because it will have a fuller meaning for us. . . . We shall try here to give a brief résumé of the kinds of wood most commonly used in furniture and why each one is put to use in its own particular way. We must begin, of course, with oak.

OAK is the oldest, most worthy, and soundest of woods. It seems actually to improve with age, becoming black and as hard as marble. It has been used all over the continent of Europe from time immemorial, but it is most typical of England, where it has become a national symbol. "Hearts of oak" have been sung by the British poets from Chaucer down to the present hour. Oak is of very slow growth and is the hardest of all woods. It is full of knots because there is so little progress made between the branches which fall off and leave a scar. It can be carved and joined but it is very difficult to turn because the hardness of the wood dulls the chisel, but once it has been cut it stays "put" forever. The most elaborate and beautiful of English oak furniture was made during the Elizabethan and Jacobean periods. Quartered oak means that the tree trunk has been sawed, not into planks but down through the

ANTIQUES

centre, criss-cross, as you would quarter an apple. When these quarters have been sawed into thin planks they result in the matched surfaces used for panelling.

AMERICAN OAK has much the same characteristics and can be put to much the same use as English oak, but it is a faster growing tree, lighter in colour and grain, and has fewer knots.

WALNUT, while somewhat less sturdy than oak, is more elegant in appearance and yields itself more readily to use. It grows almost as slowly as oak, but straight up, which gives it a satin-like grain. When quartered it yields the most beautiful matched panelling; and walnut veneer, the wavy, lovely kind used for drawer panels and table tops, is cut from the large branches at the "crotch" where the grain is confused by the branching of the limb from the trunk. That is true of "crotch" veneer from all trees. It can be cut very thin.

BLACK WALNUT was an early substitute for oak because, not being so hard, it could be used more easily, and as oak goes black with age, black walnut closely resembled it.

PINE grows everywhere, but we feel that it is our own typical tree. It was used abundantly by the earliest American settlers for common household furniture, chests, tables, etc. It is a most useful wood, growing a grand big trunk that can be used for anything from beams to buttons. It has only one bad quality—it is a soft wood. Even at that it is durable because of the large amount of resin or oil that it contains. Because of its width it is used for broad surfaces such as table tops, chair seats, etc., where no particular resiliency or toughness is required. While it is not decorative or beautiful, pine is probably the most useful wood in the world. Early pine furniture was almost always painted, and when scraped is a lovely pale yellow, sometimes mistaken for maple.

MAPLE is an out-and-out characteristically American tree, and most beautiful it is, too. Since it grew abundantly on every hillside and in every valley and had to be cut down to make way for the fields, it was very much used for every kind of furniture by our early forefathers. Chairs, tables, cupboards, high-boys, desks were all made in maple. Perhaps because it was so common people got tired of the sight of it, for most early pieces were painted. Scraping the paint off early maple is one of the never-ending jobs of the antique collector to-day, for we love maple in its natural colour, a golden yellow, soft with time.

CURLY MAPLE—We have been speaking so far of the plain maple, but there is another kind that, when finished, displays a mottled pebbly appearance that is very lovely. Antique lovers are divided into two groups: those who adore curly maple furniture and those who adore the plain. The plain is the older and the curly, perhaps, the lovelier. Curly maple was often used with the plain as a veneer, and when you have a piece like that you cannot help being satisfied. In later pieces, during Sheraton's time, it was often used with mahogany, which resulted in a most enchanting effect, purely American. Maple furniture of either sort is never found abroad, so that any bit of maple in a piece is indisputable evidence that it was made over here.

CHERRY, too, was commonly used in early American furniture. In fact, every sort of handy wood that happened to grow around the farm was utilized in that home-made furniture, resulting sometimes in the queerest combinations. Early cherry furniture, like the maple, was usually painted, and we can scrape that, too, for its colour, a warm rich red between maple and mahogany, is most pleasing.

BIRCH, HICKORY, AND ASH—all small trees—were used for turnings, spindles, chair legs, etc., where tensile strength without bulk was needed. "Tough as hickory" is an old expression, and hickory walking-sticks and golf clubs are the straightest and strongest that can be found. The delicate spindles for Windsor chairs were made of hickory. Ash, which is just about as strong, is bendable and was used for the top rails of Windsor chairs, etc. Ash, which has a long, fibrous grain, will not turn without splitting, but both birch and hickory will yield to turning and were much used for legs.

MAHOGANY—Now we have come to the most popular and in many respects the grandest wood of all. It was not used in America before the middle of the 18th Century, and was very little used in England before that time. Luckily it came along just when Chippendale did, about 1750, for what he would have done without it we cannot guess. It is a semi-tropical wood, the finest kind growing in the West Indies, the "Santo Domingo" mahogany we hear so much about. Mahogany has every possible quality that the cabinet maker could desire. It is sufficiently hard to withstand wear, as in table tops and other flat surfaces, strong enough to resist weight (think of the delicate legs on high-boys), yet it is pliable and easily worked. It carves perfectly even in the tiniest detail. It takes inlay. It can be cut into the thinnest veneer. It has a perfectly smooth close grain and polishes to perfection. It comes in numerous grades and colours, from almost as light as maple to a very rich dark, well—mahogany. It takes stain easily. In fact, it is and does everything under the sun that the cabinet maker could desire. Is it any wonder Chippendale and Phyfe both loved it so?

Mahogany, because it is so wonderful and popular, is very much imitated nowadays in baser woods, stained to look something like it, but any one with half an eye can recognize the real wood, especially the old stuff with its glorious *patine*, in half a second. Just now there is a sort of rage among antique collectors for the earlier pieces in native woods, before mahogany got over here, which is quite natural, especially for us here in America, for after all, mahogany isn't own own wood—nor anybody's—but, just the same, mahogany will hold its own against all comers, always.

CEDAR is another wood that we must mention, although we do not run into it very often among antiques. However, cedar chests were made and chests were lined with cedar, just as they are to-day, because of the perfume of the wood and its protective quality against moths.

EBONY, TULIP, PEAR, APPLE, BOX, HOLLY, GUM, etc., are among the purely decorative woods used for inlay and marquetry, and in some cases as veneer. Apple and pear also were used to some extent in whole pieces of furniture such as chests, and not infrequently we find them combined with other woods as table tops. But these are exceptions and come under the head of the odd pieces made around the farm about which we have already spoken.

English Oak

X Y Z

Gather up the fragments that remain, that nothing be lost.

JOHN: VI-2.

"X" MAY very well stand for the prices we pay for the "Antiques" we have been talking about, for "X" it is, an unknown quantity! What you pay for Antiques depends entirely on how and where you buy them. Of course, if you have plenty of money and are looking for rare pieces it is best to go to some reliable dealer and let him do the worrying. This is not much fun, but it is the only way, nowadays, to get hold of really fine pieces. Gone are the days when miracles were revealed in the barn and marvels unearthed in the attic. Of course there are still occasional rare exceptions but they are too chancey for the amateur to depend upon. Most really fine pieces are already in the hands of the dealers, or owned privately and are not for sale. Every one of these pieces is known by name, like the rare jewels of the world, and their existence is about as secret as the life of a gold fish. If such are the pieces you are after you will pay for them just what the dealer believes you can stagger under, for if you cannot pay he knows the next man can. The prices of these pieces are fantastic and sentimental. Money becomes as naught in exchange for rarities.

All up and down the Atlantic seaboard in the large cities and sometimes in historic villages there are reliable dealers, not many of them, to be sure, but they make up in integrity what they lack in numbers. In no business in the world is a reputation for integrity more valuable than in dealing in antiques. These men are as easy to locate as are reliable jewellers or other dealers in high-class commodities. Such a dealer will find what you want—in time—and when you get it you can depend upon it being what you pay for—and you will pay a thumping big price, too.

That is the logical, sensible way to go about collecting fine antiques to-day. It is the only safe way.

Another fairly good way, but full of pitfalls, is to follow the auciton sales in large cities. Sometimes fine collections are disposed of in this way, but not nearly so often as the advertisements would have you think. Usually such sales, even under the cloak of a great name, are no more than the disposition of "seconds," doubtful or ordinary pieces, that the collector is anxious to get rid of. Few are the souls, indeed, that can resist the temptation of selling to a public eager to throw away money regardless of value. You will find few dealers at such sales, and those who are there to watch the market walk out with a shrug.

But occasionally there is a real, authentic great sale of rare antiques. Then you have the professional buyers to compete with and if you get a piece it is simply because you have paid too much for it. They let you have it rather than chance selling it to you later on. So auction sales are pretty hazardous places for the amateur to wander into. Fascinating, of course, and much more fun than buying from a dealer. But do not deceive yourself into thinking you will find bargains there!

The next way to buy antiques is to drift into the little out-of-the way shops on side streets. It is practically impossible to find a genuine fine or rare piece in such a place, although fakes will be thick enough. These small men know as well as the big ones the value of a good piece, and if by chance they do stumble on a "find" they are almost certain to take it to a dealer "higher up" who will at once give them a fair price for it, and be done with it. They are in-between men. Of course unimportant stuff such as the big fellows would not handle is found in such places, and if you are a simple collector with not much money and are a fair judge of values you may find many a nice little piece in such a shop. But here, too, the price will depend upon how much you know of values and on how much the dealer thinks he can make out of you. This kind of collecting is, of course, what most of us indulge in, and experience is the only thing that can help you there.

Another and the most blissful way to find antiques is to look for them in the country at the original source. We have explained elsewhere how slim the pickings are nowadays, but if you are lucky enough to live in a likely neighbourhood, which means somewhere in New England or thereabouts,

ANTIQUES

and are amiable and patient with your neighbours, you may find really good things, and at a trifle of cost. Country auctions are a source of very real bargains sometimes but here, too, knowledge of what you are getting, the ability to recognize what you see, is invaluable. But, oh, the thrill when you do see it; the joy, tinged with sympathy and humility, when at last the precious old thing leaves the hands that have cherished it so long and comes to yours! Real collectors, real lovers of old things do not gloat at such a moment. They may afterward, but not then; not in front of the old house whose dust-glazed eyes gaze desperately into the trampled garden. They drive home quietly with the treasure in their arms.

That, of course, is the ideal way to find antiques, for then you truly love them, and, while it is rare that a very great piece is found that way, many dear and homely things can still be picked up in the country. Look for them there. Learn, at any rate, the soil from which they come.

"Y", if you will permit a pun at this late date, might stand for why we buy antiques, anyway! The first impulse would be to say because we are sentimental, but while sentiment does indeed play a very large part in it, there is a good foundation of Yankee common sense beneath it. American antiques are valuable and they will become more valuable as time goes on. They have been a gold mine for those far-sighted persons, sentimental or otherwise, who had the good judgment to buy them years ago. No wildcat oil venture ever paid such returns on the original investment as have some of those early finds. Of course, like all popular booms, antiques have in many cases suffered from inflation. Many enthusiastic buyers could not, if they would, get back what they have paid for some pieces. But at least they could get something back, which is more than can be said of factory-made stuff. There will always be a market, and a good one, too, for antiques. Entirely aside from any other consideration, antiques, carefully purchased, are a good "buy."

"Z"—and we have come to the end. We have tried, as we said we would, to cover the subject of American Antiques broadly and briefly, but now that it is finished we find that, of all we hoped to say, very little has been written. There is so much more; so many things have been reluctantly put aside. This is no more than a nibble, after all. But if interest has been quickened, if the reader wants now to follow up, in bigger and more comprehensive books than this, the subjects touched upon here, if the old things that belonged to our forefathers in the early days of our country's life have come out of the dim shadows to stand a little nearer to him, then the main object of our task has been fulfilled, and we can lay it aside with the grateful feeling that it has not been done in vain.

THE END

BIBLIOGRAPHY

THE PRACTICAL BOOK OF PERIOD FURNITURE	H. D. Eberlein and A. McClure
FURNITURE OF OUR FOREFATHERS	Esther Singleton
FURNITURE OF THE OLDEN TIME	Frances Clary Morse
COLONIAL FURNITURE IN AMERICA	Luke Vincent Lockwood
FURNITURE OF THE PILGRIM CENTURY	Wallace Nutting
EARLY AMERICAN CRAFTSMEN	Walter A. Dyer
HANDBOOK OF FURNITURE STYLES	Walter A. Dyer
STYLE IN FURNITURE	R. Davis Benn
FURNITURE MASTERPIECES OF DUNCAN PHYFE	Charles Over Cornelius
HOME LIFE IN COLONIAL DAYS	Alice Morse Earle
OLD GLASS	Mrs. N. Hudson Moore
STIEGEL GLASS	Frederick William Hunter
AMERICAN GLASSWARE	Edwin Atlee Barber
SANDWICH GLASS	Leonore Wheeler Williams
COLONIAL LIGHTING	Arthur H. Hayward
HISTORIC SILVER OF THE COLONIES	Francis Hill Bigelow
OLD PLATE	John Henry Buck
AMERICAN SILVER OF THE 17TH AND 18TH CENTURIES	C. Louise Avery
OLD PEWTER	Malcolm Bell
AMERICAN PEWTER	J. B. Kerfoot
THE OLD CLOCK BOOK	Mrs. N. Hudson Moore
OLD CLOCKS AND WATCHES	F. J. Britten
THE CRAFT OF HAND-MADE RUGS	Amy Mali Hicks
A BOOK OF HAND-WOVEN COVERLETS	Eliza Calvert Hall
QUILTS	Marie D. Webster
THE DEVELOPMENT OF EMBROIDERY IN AMERICA	Candace Wheeler
AMERICAN SAMPLERS	E. S. Bolton and E. J. Coe
CHATS ON OLD LACE AND NEEDLEWORK	Emily Leigh Lowes

BIBLIOGRAPHY

ART IN NEEDLEWORK	*Lewis F. Day* and *Mary Buckle*
DICTIONARY OF NEEDLEWORK	*Cauldfield and Saward*
HISTORIC TEXTILE FABRICS	*Richard Glazier*
THE CHINTZ BOOK	*MacIver Percival*
ANTIQUES—THEIR RESTORATION AND PRESERVATION	*Alfred Lucas*
THE GENTLE ART OF FAKING	*Riccardi Nobili*

INDEX

INDEX

INDEX

Adam, Robert, his influence on English furniture, 3; his designs executed in Hepplewhite's shop, 22; his influence on Hepplewhite, 53; his approach to the sideboard, 114.
Andirons, and their use, 56.
"Angel" bed, 8.
Apple-wood, 147.
Ash, 145.
Auction sales, 148.

Backs, various forms of; see Chairs, 14–26.
Bagnell, early Boston clock maker, 32.
Balboa mirror, 73.
Ball foot, 13.
Bandy, or cabriole, leg, 13.
Banister backs on chairs, 15, 16.
Banjo clocks, 33.
Bayberry candles, 63.
Beakers, an early form of drinking cup, 119.
"Beaufett," or corner cupboard, 31.
Bed hangings, crewel work, 97; tufted and knotted, 97.
Bed quilts and coverlets, 96; coverlets, their patterns and names, 98; quilts, patchwork and piecework, 99; padded and corded, 101.
Bedposts, the changing types, 7.
Bedsteads, evolution from the ancient type, 5; early American, 6; "Presse," 6; "Field" or "Tent," 6; Chippendale, 6; "Half-headed," 7; "Sleigh," 7; "Spool," 7; "Trundle," 8; "Angel," 8.
Beeswax, to prepare for polishing, 105.
Benn, 114.
Bennington Pottery, its history, etc., 69.
Betty lamps, 65.
Bible boxes, 35.
"Big Four," Chippendale, Adam, Hepplewhite, and Sheraton, 11.
Birch, 145.
Bookcases, 38.
Boston rockers, 17.
Boxwood, 147.
Brasses, or mounts, for furniture, 75.
Brewster, Deacon, his fine turned chair, 15.
"Bunker Hill," Sandwich glass cup plates, 49.
Bureaus, 9.
Butterfly hinge, 58.
Butterfly table, 130.
Buying of antiques, good and bad methods, 148.

Cabriole, or Dutch bandy leg, 13; of Chippendale, 20.
Calico, or printed chintz, 96.
Candle stands, 88.
Candles, 63.
Candlesticks, 64.
Canopies, in the evolution from ancient beds, 5; in the "Tent" bed, 6.
Card tables, Phyfe's, 139.
Card and tea tables, of Hepplewhite and Sheraton, 135.
Care and restoration of antiques, 102ff.
Carver chair, 15.
Caudle cups, 118.
Cedar, 146.
Cellaret, 116.
Chair tables, 128.
Chairs, most versatile of the furniture family, 13; turnings, 13; Dutch bandy or cabriole leg, 13; straight leg of Hepplewhite and Sheraton, 14; of Chippendale, 20; curved leg of Phyfe, 14; the top rail, 14; splat, or fiddle back, 14, 15; slat back, 14, 16; banister back, 15, 16; Windsor back, 15, 16; Carver chair, 15; Boston rockers, 17; Hitchcock chair, 18; Empire, 18; Chippendale backs, 20; ladder backs, 20; roundabouts, 21; Hepplewhite backs, 21; shield back, 22; heart back, 22; Sheraton backs, 24; Phyfe backs, 25; medallion back, 26.
Cherry, 145.
Chests, the oldest form of furniture, 27; the Connecticut chest, 27; the Hadley chest, 28; the tall-boy, 28; the high-boy, 29; the low-boy, 29; the chest-on-chest, 29.
Chests of drawers, 9.
Chintz, history of, 97.
Chippendale, the most outstanding figure in history of furniture making, 11; his Cupid's bow top rail, 14; his chair backs, 20, 21; how to recognize his furniture, 21; his fine secretary desks, 36; his mirror designs, 73; his footstools, 87; his fire screens, 87; his candle stands, 89; his settee, 111; he built no sideboards, 114; his tripod table, 131; his card tables, 132; his other tables, 133.
Chippendale bed, with carved footposts, 6.
Chocolate-pots, 119.
Classic Urn, 3.
Clock makers, Willard, Terry, Thomas, and Hoadley, 33.

INDEX

Clocks, 32; tall clocks and their makers, 32; banjo clocks, 33; Terry clock, 34.
"Cock's Head" hinge, 58.
Coffee-pots, 119.
"Colonial Pillar" andirons, 56.
Colour, difficulties in dyeing materials in early days, 82.
Connecticut chest, 27.
"Constitution" mirror, 43, 72.
Copper lustre, 69.
Corner cupboard, 30; how made and used, 31.
Cornucopia sofa, 113.
Counterpanes, 97.
Coverlets, 96; their patterns and names, 98; patchwork and piecework quilts, 99; padded and corded, 101.
Crewel-work, 81.
Crewel-work bed hangings, 97.
Cromwellian period and its furniture, 61.
Cup plates of Sandwich glass, 49.
Cupboards, 30.
Curly maple, 145.
Curule leg, 39; of Duncan Phyfe, 14, 139; of Adam, 14.

Dealers, dependence on, in procuring antiques, 148.
Desks, evolution from a slant-top box, 35; the drop-front desk, 35; the secretary desk, 36; Hepplewhite's and Sheraton's secretaries, 37; bookcases, 38; knee-hole desks, 38; Empire desks, 38.
Dining tables, of Hepplewhite and Sheraton, 134; of Phyfe, 139.
"Dish top" table of Chippendale, 132.
Door knockers, 58.
Draperies, 5, 7.
Dressing glass, 9.
Drop-front desk, 35.
Dyeing, difficulties in obtaining colours in early days, 82.

"Eagle" Sandwich glass cup plates, 49.
"Easy chairs," 21.
Ebony, 147.
Electric lighting, its introduction in New York, 66.
Embroidery, as taught by the Moravians, 84; embroidery on white, 85.
Empire chairs, 18.

Empire desks, 38.
Empire lamps, 66.
Empire mirrors, 73.
Empire period, 39; American Empire, 40.
Empire sofas, 113.
Extension dining tables, of Sheraton and Hepplewhite, 134; of Phyfe, 139.

Fakes and reproductions, 41.
Feet: ball, Flemish scroll, Spanish, and Dutch, 13; ball-and-claw, snakes' head, and spade, 14.
Fiddle-back, or splat-back chairs, 14, 15.
Field bed, or "Tent" bed, 6.
Finishing, the process of the old furniture makers, 104.
Fire screens, 87.
Fireplace fittings and their use, 56.
Flemish scroll foot, 13.
Footstools, 86.
Four-poster bed, its evolution, 5.
Franklin, Benjamin, inventor of the rocking chair, 16.
Franklin stoves, 57.
Fret backs, Chippendale's, 21.
Furnishing of old beds, 7.

"Garland" door knocker, 58.
Gas, its introduction for lighting purposes, 66.
Gate-leg table, 129.
"Gentleman and Cabinet Maker's Director, The," Chippendale's book of designs, 19.
Girandole, 74.
Glass, history of, 45; Wistar, 46; "South Jersey," 46; Stiegel, 47; Sandwich, 48.
Glass candlesticks, 64.
Glass lamps, 66.
Graves, Richard, an early pewterer, 94.
Greatback, Daniel, designer of the popular Bennington pottery figures, 69.
Gum wood, 147.

"H" hinge, 58.
Hadley chest, 28.
Hair-work of the Victorian era, 141.
"Half-headed" bed, 7.
Hall marks on early silver, 122.
"Hammer" door knocker, 58.
Hangings, bed, crewel work, and tufted and knotted, 97.

INDEX

Hardware, its manufacture and use in Colonial times, 55.
"Harrison" cup plates of Sandwich glass, 49.
"Henry Clay" cup plates of Sandwich glass, 49.
Hepplewhite, the man and his work, 53; bureaus, or "chests of drawers," 9; straight chair leg, 14; his furniture as distinguished from Sheraton's, 22; chair backs, 22; chair seats, and legs, 23; secretary desks, 37; bookcase desks, 38; introduces process of japanning, 62; mirrors, 73; candle stands, 89; settees, 111; sideboards, 114, 115; tables, 134ff.
Hepplewhite, Alice, 53, 107.
"Hessian" andirons, 56.
Hickory, 145.
High-boy, 29.
Hinges, 57.
Hitchcock chair, 18.
Holly wood, 147.
Hooked rugs, 60.
Horse screens, 88.
Hound pitchers, distinction between the "Jersey" and "Bennington," 69.
Hull, John, silversmith, 122.
Hurricane glasses, candle shields, 64.

Jacobean period and its furniture, 61.
Japanning and lacquering, 62.

Kas, the Pennsylvania Dutch cupboard or wardrobe, 31.
Kerosene lamps, introduction of, 66.
Kidney table, of Sheraton, 137.
Knee-hole desks, 38.
Knockers, 58.

Lace glass, of the Sandwich factory, 49.
Lacquering and japanning, 62.
Ladder backs, or slat-back chairs, 14, 16; Chippendale's, 20.
Ladies' writing tables, 38.
Lafayette, or courting, mirror, 73.
Lamps, of the Colonists, 63; Betty lamps, 65; pewter, 65; glass, 66; Empire, 66; kerosene, 66.
Legs, Dutch, bandy, or cabriole, 13; straight, 14, 20, 23; reeded, 14, 114, 137; curule, 14, 39, 139; pillar-and-claw, 113, 140.
Lighting, lamps and candles, 63.
Linseed oil, in polishing, 105.
"Lion's Head" door knocker, 58.

Looking-glasses, or mirrors: hung above bureaus, 9; their history, 71; walnut, 71; Constitution, 43, 72; Empire, 73; Courting, 73; Girandoles, 74.
Low-boy, 29.
Lustreware, 67; pink, 68; Sunderland, 68; silver "resist," 68; copper, 68.
Lyre-back chairs, of Duncan Phyfe, 25.

Mahogany, as used by Chippendale, 20; by Savery, 29; by Phyfe, 91; introduction of, 146; uses of, 146.
Maple, 145.
Medallion chair back, 26.
Mirrors, 9; their history, 71; walnut, 71; Constitution, 72; Empire, 73; Courting, 73; Girandoles, 74.
Mixing table and cellaret, 116.
Moravian work, fine embroidery, 84.
Mounts, or brasses, for furniture, 75.
Mugs, in early silverware, 120.

Napoleon, his influence on the French taste and Empire furniture, 39.
Needlework, of our foremothers, 79; early European samplers, 80; American samplers, 81; crewel work, 81; Turkey-work, 82; needlework tapestry, 83; Moravian work, 83; embroidery on white, 85; crewel-work bed hangings, 97; tufted and knotted hangings, 97.
Needlework tapestry, 83.
Norton, John, first maker of Bennington pottery, 69.

Oak, quartered, 143; in furniture making, 143; difference between the English and American woods, 144.
Occasional pieces, in furniture, 86; footstools, 86; fire screens, 87.
Oil, whale, 65; kerosene, 66; linseed, 105.

Padded and corded quilts, 100.
Paint, the removal of, 103, 145.
Painted furniture, of Adam, 3; of Hepplewhite and Sheraton, 23, 134.
Patchwork and piecework quilts, 99.
Patina (or patine), recognition of, 43, 104; **care** of, 104; restoration of, 105.
Pear wood, 147.
Pembroke table, 136.

INDEX

Pewter, 93ff.
Pewter lamps, 65.
Phyfe, Duncan, the man and his work, 90; table and chair legs, 14; chair backs, 25; his work in relation to Adam and Sheraton, 25; America's greatest cabinet maker, 26; forced to succumb to the coarse Empire styles, 39; tables, 138ff.
Pictures in needlework: needlework tapestry, 83; Moravian work, 83.
Pie-crust table, 132.
Pier, or console, tables, of Hepplewhite and Sheraton, 135.
Pillar-and-claw dining table, 140.
Pine, 144.
Pineapple decoration, 7.
Pink lustre, 68.
Pitchers, lustre, 67, 68; "hound," 69.
Plates, cup, of Sandwich glass, 49.
Pole screens, 88.
Polish, liquid, how remove, 103.
Polishing, how done, 105.
Political symbols, in glass bottles, etc., 48, 49.
Porringers, 120.
Pottery, Bennington, its history, etc., 69.
"Presse" beds, 6.
"Presse" cupboard, 30, 128.
Prices, to be paid for antiques, 148.

Quartered oak, how sawn, 143.
Quilts, 96; coverlets, their patterns and names, 98; patchwork and piecework, 99; padded and corded, 101.

Refectory table, 128.
Reproductions, 41.
Restoration and care of antiques, 102ff.
Restoration period, and its furniture, 61.
Revere, Paul, silversmith and patriot, 122.
Rocking chair, 16; Boston rocker, 17.
Roll-top desk, 37.
Roundabout chairs, Chippendale's, 21.
Rugs, hooked, their origin and the various designs, 60.

Samplers, Early European, 80; American, 81.
Sandwich glass, 48.
Satin-wood, 3, 107.
Savery, William, Philadelphia, cabinet maker, 29.
Secret drawers, in early desks, 36. 38.

Secretary desk, 36; Hepplewhite's designs compared to Sheraton's, 37.
Settee, the double chair form, 110; Chippendale settees, 111; Hepplewhite settees, 111; Sheraton settees, 112.
Settle, 110.
Shearer, Thomas, first designer of sideboards, 144.
Sheraton, Thomas, the man and his work, 107ff; his bureaus, or "chest of drawers," 9; "dressing glasses," 9; reeded chair leg, 14; furniture as distinguished from Hepplewhite's, 22; his genius for proportion and unfailing good taste, 23; chair backs, 24; chair legs, 25; his comment on the early type of desk, 35; secretary desks, 37; footstools, 87; pole screens, horse screens, 88; candle stands, 89; settees and sofas, 112; sideboards, 114, 115; tables, 134ff.
Sideboards, 114; Hepplewhite sideboard, 115; Sheraton sideboard, 115; Empire sideboards, 116.
Silver "resist," a variety of lustreware, 68.
Silverware, high quality of the early forms, 117; beakers, 117; tankards, 148; mugs, 118; caudle cups, 118; porringers, 118; tea, coffee, and chocolate pots, 119; spoons, 119; how early silverware was made, 120; some of the great Colonial silversmiths, 122ff.
Slat-back, or ladder-back chairs, 14, 16.
"Sleigh" bed, 7.
Sofa tables, 136.
Sofas, 110; Sheraton sofas, 112; Empire sofas, 113; Victorian sofas, 113.
"South Jersey" glass, 46.
Spade foot, 14, 23.
Spanish foot, 13.
"Sparking lamp," 66.
Spinning wheels, 82.
Splat-back or fiddle-back chairs, 14, 15.
"Spool" bed, 7.
Spoons, 119.
Spots, to remove, 105.
"Spread Eagle" door knocker, 58.
Staffordshire, 70.
Standish, Loara, her sampler, 81.
"Steeple Top" pattern of andirons, 56.
Stiegel, "Baron," 46ff.
Stiegel Glass, 47.
Stoves, the Franklin, 57.
Sunderland lustre, 68.

INDEX

Tables, 127; "table bords," 127; trestle tables, 127; refectory tables, 128; chair tables, 128; gate-leg tables, 129; butterfly table, 130; other early tables, 130; Chippendale tripod, 131; Chippendale card, dining, and other tables, 132, 133; Hepplewhite and Sheraton tables, 134; extension dining table, 134; pier or console tables, 135; card and tea tables, 135; Pembroke table, 136; sofa tables, 136; Sheraton "kidney" table, 137; Sheraton work tables, 138; Martha Washington work table, 138; Phyfe dining, card, and work tables, 139; pillar-and-claw dining table, 140; Empire work tables, 140.
Tall-boy, or high-boy, 28, 29.
Tall clocks, and their makers, 32.
Tambour desks, 37.
Tankards, 118.
Tea-pots, 119.
Tea tables and table stands, 130.
Temperature, effect of, on old furniture, 106.
"Tent" or "Field" beds of Colonial times, 6.
Terry, Eli, 33.
Terry clocks, 34.
"Tippecanoe" pattern, in Sandwich glass, 49.
Toile de Jouy, where and when made, 97.
Top rail, of the early chairs, 14.
Trestle tables, 127.
Trundle beds, 8.
Tufted and knotted bed hangings, 97.
Tulip wood, 147.
Turkey-work, 82.
Turnings, 13.
Two-seated, or wagon, chair, 16.

Valance, 5.
Varnish, in japanning, 62; the removal of, 103.
Victorian era, 141.

Wagon chairs, 16.
Wainscot chair, 15.
Wall clocks, 32.
Walnut, 144.
Walnut mirrors, 71.
Washington, George, bequeaths his tambour secretary, 37; inventor of a wine-bottle coaster, 116.
Waxing and polishing, how done, 105.
Whale oil, as fuel for lamps, 65.
Willard, Simon, 32, 33.
Windsor backs, on chairs, 15, 16.
Windsor chairs, 16; source of the name, 17.
Wistar, Caspar, first glass factory in America, 46.
Wooden clock works, 34.
Woods, in their relation to furniture, 143.
Work tables, Sheraton's and Hepplewhite's, 137; the Martha Washington, 138; Phyfe's, 139; under the Empire influence, 140.
Writing tables, ladies', 38.

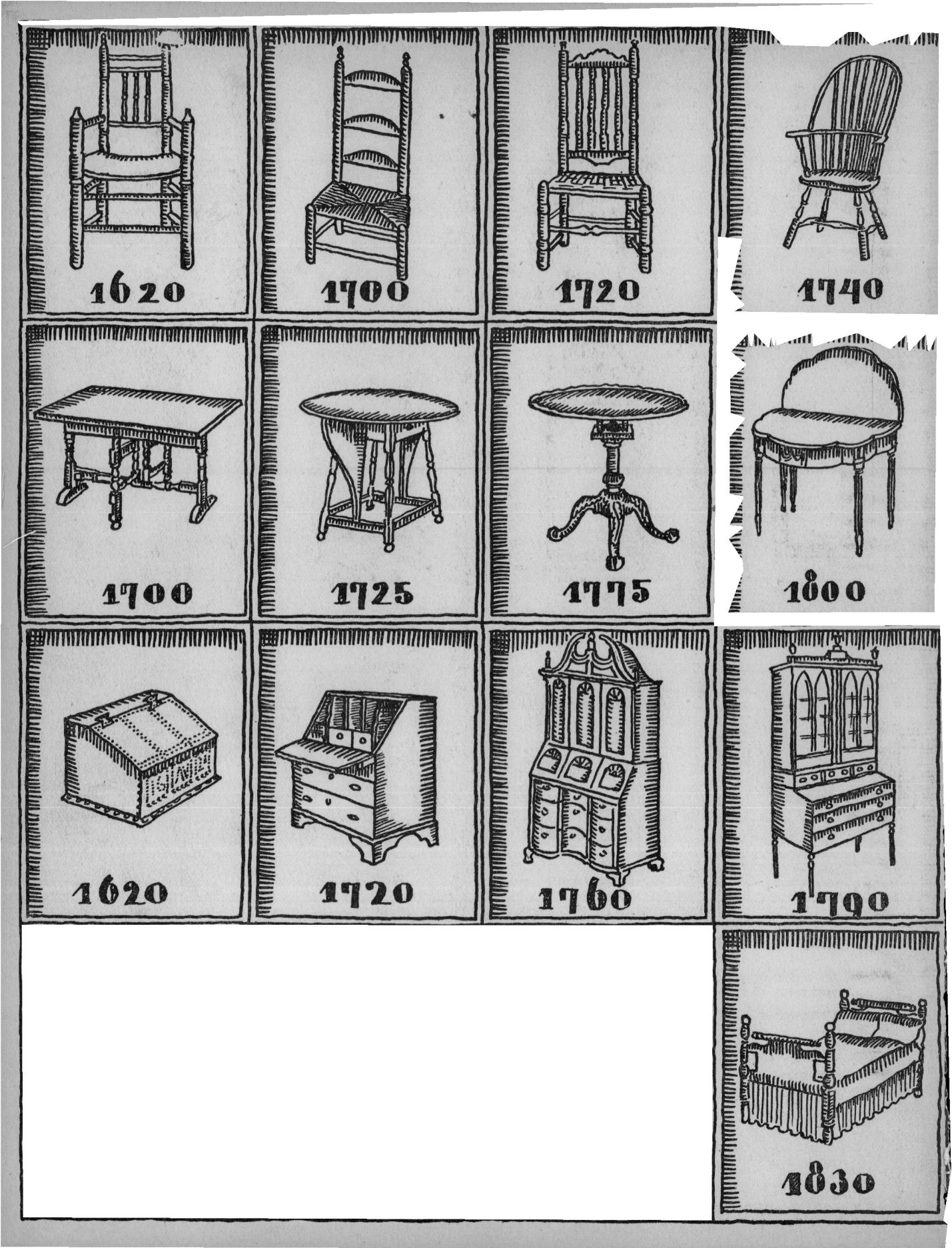

1620	1700	1720	1740
1700	1725	1775	1800
1620	1720	1760	1790
			1830